ANGEL OF THE STORM
The Mysterious Path of an NYPD Cop

By
Ben Reiver

Angel of the Storm © Copyright 2025 by Ben Reiver

All rights reserved.

No part of this publication may be reproduced, distributed, or transmitted in any form or by any means, including photocopying, recording, or other electronic or mechanical methods, without the prior written permission of the publisher, except as permitted by U.S. copyright law.

For permission requests, contact ben@angelofthestorm.com

Cover Art by Tony Ko

Edited by Cassie Lennox

First Hardcover Edition September 2025

ISBN 979-8-218-76464-7

To all of those sent to me in my storm and theirs.

Contents

Prologue 1
PART I 3
   Chapter 1: The Green Orb 5
   Chapter 2: Stranger in Town 9
   Chapter 3: The Apple & The Tree 15
   Chapter 4: Woodland 19
   Chapter 5: Peace Through Strength 27
   Chapter 6: Intermezzo 33
PART II 41
   Chapter 7: Master of None 43
   Chapter 8: Pillar to Post 51
   Chapter 9: The Golden Gloves 59
   Chapter 10: September 11, 2001 67
   Chapter 11: Talk the Talk 73
   Chapter 12: Walk the Walk 77
   Chapter 13: The Actual Hangover 83
PART III 89
   Chapter 14: The Wool Suit 91
   Chapter 15: Vapor Lock 95
   Chapter 16: The Police Academy 99
   Chapter 17: Into the Dark 107
   Chapter 18: The Final Test 111

Chapter 19: The Devil Wears Nada 115

PART IV 121

Chapter 20: Hot Cocoa 123

Chapter 21: Snake in the Grass... 127

Chapter 22: I Know That Name... 133

Chapter 23: Interfaith Rabbi 139

Chapter 24: Area 100.. 143

Chapter 25: Rough Seas... 153

PART V 161

Chapter 26: The Guide.. 163

Chapter 27: A Date With Special Ops................................171

Chapter 28: Harbor Charlie 177

Chapter 29: Hurricane Irene 189

Chapter 30: The Aftermath 203

Chapter 31: Little Fire 209

Epilogue 217

Prologue

"God and the Universe have given you a mission only you were born to do.

Just like explorers of the past setting sail into the vast unknown, your soul is doing the same. You have been given a ship, a crew, just enough food to survive, and just enough resources to keep the journey going.

Your days will range from exciting adventures to extreme boredom. There will be times when your journey is filled with an abundance of treasure. Other times you will have no wind to push the sails, and it feels as if you're going nowhere. However, the current is still moving you in a direction.

There will be storms, and there will be rough seas. There will be sunshine and calm waters; time used to repair your ship with patches, nails, anything you can find. You'll have to toil in bilge up to your knees and move heavy stones around, so that the ballast is just right for the next challenge ahead.

Your crew will be the best one minute, then grumble behind your back with every unpopular decision you make. There will be mutinies you'll have to put down, and even force some you've known all journey, to walk the plank; but it's your ship and your ship only.

Stay on the ship long enough and you will see some of your crew leave. Some couldn't handle the journey, some died in battle, some in accidents, and some by illness; but the ship keeps moving, because God and the Universe are pulling you in a direction of their choosing.

ANGEL OF THE STORM

With all these wonderful stories, tales of adventure, personal victories, sad sonnets of loss, and lost spaces in between, it is still your ship and your ship only.

Then when you get to the end of the journey and it is revealed where you went, how long it took, and why, you'll look back and understand the reason why it was so difficult.

Your soul was being prepared for the next adventure."

Ben Reiver

Retired NYPD Special Operations

PART I

Chapter 1: The Green Orb

My memory gets weaker as time flows by and past battles take a physical toll on the mind. It's quite sad since my ability to recall the most minute details from infancy to a few years ago, was quite extraordinary. However, the one story etched in my mind, is how I became the instrument of a miracle for others. I never thought that I would be chosen for such a task, but my dad was right when he said to me once, "You might not save the world, but you might save *someone's* world."

Born in Far Rockaway, Queens, NY, and into a blue-collar family, we quickly moved to Rosedale, Queens when I was an infant. Most of my young childhood was spent there before moving out to Long Island, NY. The house in Rosedale was simple, but the backyard was huge compared to most homes in Queens. It was big enough to have a pool, and the neighbors on the other side of the fence used to throw candy into it as a game. My dad would go out every week to check it out, and when I heard him cursing, I knew those kids hit their mark.

The house screamed early to mid 1970s. Ugly wallpaper with brown, orange, and metallic tones, met shaggy carpet and dark wood furniture. We had an 8-track stereo upstairs in the living room, and an old reel-to-reel tape player downstairs that used to hypnotize me with its motion. The black and white checkered floor of the basement would flood on occasion. This was due to us being near the marsh and below the water table. The loud whining sound of the shop-vac would scare the crap out of me when the water had to be vacuumed up.

Nothing was louder than the passenger jets, though. We lived so close to JFK airport, you could probably throw a rock and hit a runway. The planes flew low enough to see passengers in the windows. Whenever the Concorde took off or came in on final approach, the entire house would shake. Windows would rattle to the point where it felt like an earthquake. It was such an awesome sight, and I'd smile ear-to-ear each time.

I learned how to read by watching those jets on the front porch. It was my hobby as a very young boy. You could put me out there all day and I wouldn't move. I'd point towards the planes and yell out as each one flew by, "TWA! PAN AM! EASTERN!" These companies have been gone for decades and are just long-lost memories like Rosedale.

Although old and run down, the house had some magic left in her. We didn't have much money back then as a young family. With my dad being a NYC cop, my mom could only work part time to juggle the responsibilities at home. My sister and I had our own bedrooms, but I had the hand-me-down furniture. One of those hand-me-downs was her old crib. It was on its last legs, mostly due to my part.

I was a big baby, weighing in at almost 10 pounds. I'm not sure what happened after that, because I wound up being one of the smallest kids in school until I was 14 years old. Nonetheless, I was a big, strong, chunky baby. I remember almost every night, all night, standing up and rocking the crib with my hands around the wood beams as if I were in prison. My dad tried and tried to keep that crib together as it fell apart. Twine, nails, screws, tape, and glue, were no match for my brawn.

THE GREEN ORB

It came to the point where I could no longer be in the crib due to it being condemned by the Department of Buildings, so I went into a bed at a very early age. If this happened nowadays, people would be screaming and child services would be at the door, but this was the 1970s. We were built a little tougher and our parents gave less of a concern about safety. It's really where the story begins. Had it not been for low income at the time, a rickety crib, and a fat baby, I don't know how it starts or where it goes.

One thing I don't remember is my dad's exact schedule. I think at the time he was on what they called the "9 squad chart". This meant he would do a rotating week of days, a week of nights, a week of midnights, and rotating days off. All I know is that I hardly saw him. He was either sleeping or at work, with little time in between. Maybe it was too much for my mom to handle the workload at home, but it was very isolating for me until a special visitor showed up.

Being in bed so young without anything to physically keep me on it, was a recipe for a problem since babies like to roll. I was no different, and I wound up rolling off the bed one night. I sat there on the floor and stared down the hallway towards my parent's room, but nobody was coming. I couldn't cry either, because the fall knocked the wind out of me.

Once I got my wind back, I was entranced by a humming sound. My attention turned to the wall which had a window and an electric socket underneath it. The sound emanated from the wall, and a small green light about the size of a tennis ball emerged from it. The light remained stationary for a bit as the humming sound began to lessen; then it slowly came toward me.

I remained calm as the light enveloped me and made me feel warm. It lifted me back up onto the bed, and I quickly fell back asleep. Every night I rolled off, the green light would come out of the same spot and put me back onto the bed very gently. There were even a couple of times where I'd be on the floor playing, and it would come out of the wall for a few moments before fading away again.

After I got a little older and started sleeping better, the light didn't visit or help me anymore. I didn't know what the feeling of loss was back then, but I do remember feeling very sad not seeing it again. I felt as though whatever it was, its work was done and now I am alone. It turned out that this was not the case. The green light became part of my life and ties into everything that I am today.

Chapter 2: Stranger in Town

In the early 1980s, Rosedale was about to become a thing of the past as we embarked on a new life out on Long Island. With my sister and I getting a little bit older and easier to take care of, my mom was able to work full time, and more money came into the house. This afforded us a safer and more quiet life as we settled into East Meadow, NY.

Giant oak, maple, and birch trees lined the streets and rose up from the backyards. Dogwood, weeping willow, and crab apple trees dotted front lawns of some of the 1950s and 1960s-esque ranch-style homes of that area. The silence was deafening as the loud roar of passenger planes was replaced by a soft chirp of the occasional cricket. It was a sharp contrast compared to the concrete jungle and cratered roads of the city.

My dad was in the twilight of his career as an NYPD cop, having maybe four to five years to go before retirement. His schedule changed and he was now working steady 10am-6pm with weekends off. This is because he volunteered to walk a "beat" (foot post), and train young officers in exchange for better hours to see his family. It was what we needed, and I was finally able to see my dad for more than just an hour here or there.

The neighbors were very welcoming, and I had plenty of other kids to play with. We did the typical Long Island thing by playing catch on the lawn, fishing, fireworks on July 4th, and joining little league baseball. It was a great time for us as a family, but the honeymoon was about to come to an end for me.

When I started school, kids didn't treat me the same as others. It's because I spoke, acted, and dressed differently. I didn't fit in with the kids whose families had more money than we did. My hair was your typical and laughable 1970s bowl haircut, while most of the other boys had real haircuts. I was also on the small side physically compared to the other kids. The issues went beyond cultural and physical as hurdles that could be overcome, became illness.

I remember looking down at my hands around the age of 6, and for some reason, they felt strange. Tingling became itching, then bumps began to surface on my young hands. One at a time they popped up, became larger, and sometimes very painful. By the age of 7, there were over 100 warts big and small, all over my hands.

Unfortunately for me, it was time to start 1st grade. Kids would look at me and only see my hands. Naturally, kids could be cruel at that age. They do not have the capacity as to what or why some kids are different than others. Simply put, I was a freak and treated as such. Hardly anyone would talk to me, and sometimes verbal abuse became physical.

As time went on, the excuse of "kids being kids" faded away. It could've been dealt with by teachers and administrators, but the abuse continued. I had very few friends, and although my parents did everything they could to help me out, the medical technology wasn't there to deal with such a large problem. Three or four warts would combine into one, making any type of medication at the time useless. Plus, any surgical option was too invasive at that age.

Regardless of surgery or not, my hands were deformed, and I was disabled in every sense of the word. I could barely do the things I loved such as baseball, writing, and drawing. My hands looked very claw-like as if I were 80 years old and suffering from arthritis. I couldn't close them or open them fully due to the cracking and bleeding of the skin at almost every knuckle and joint.

At the time when boys started liking girls and passing notes, most girls ran away and said cruel things to me. It went on for years; then just before my 12th birthday, enough was enough. Despite the risks, I told my parents I wanted the surgery no matter the lasting consequences.

We went back to the doctor, and they explained the process. Back in 1988, or least where we lived, there weren't any painless laser treatments available. Also, freezing agents at the time weren't powerful enough to remove the warts. The only way to get it done was to scoop out each of the 100+ warts with a scalpel, then stitch up each hole with what little skin I had left on my small hands. To me, the abuse and isolation was more painful than any surgery could be. We scheduled the procedure for three weeks from then, shortly after Passover/Easter holiday break.

During the break, I went down to see my grandparents in Delray Beach, FL as we usually did each year once they moved there from New York. Knowing what was coming at the doctor's office in a few weeks, I did all the things I wanted to do as a kid that age as if I were going to the electric chair. I swam, went fishing, acted a fool, ate everything in sight, and joked & smiled with my Papa Lou-Lou. Most importantly, though, I prayed.

Each night at Passover dinner I prayed for some sort of miracle, because no matter how much swimming, fishing, and foolishness I did to keep my mind off it, I was still scared for what was to come. After nearly 6 years of dealing with this physical issue and not understanding why kids treated me this way, I still tried to have faith as I approached the eleventh hour.

I returned to New York and faced reality with my appointment for surgery only a week away. My head hit the pillow for my first night back home, and I couldn't sleep at all. It was a restless night filled with thoughts about the pain to come. I did my best to settle down by thinking about fishing at the lake, the calmness of the water, the grackles stealing my bread, and the joy of catching bluegills. Eventually I went to sleep, and it was some of the deepest sleep I ever had.

A humming sound jolted me awake, but when I thought I woke up, I was looking at myself sleeping. "I'm dreaming," I told myself. I was looking around my room in East Meadow, but there was a very familiar Rosedale vibe. The humming sound almost sounded like the pulsating noise from a generator. A bright green light appeared and shined from the two little windows on the far wall of my bedroom. I couldn't tell if it was coming from outside or inside, but I rolled off the bed and dropped to my knees. This was not the same reaction to the green light I had when I was a baby. There was no warmth, I didn't feel at peace, and my nearly 12-year-old brain was afraid and confused.

The sound got even louder and the light brighter. I hid my face as deep into my knees as I could and covered my ears tightly. I screamed out, "Stop!" and the bright light and ear-piercing noise vanished. It was replaced by the faint sound of a cricket outside. I woke up in a cold sweat, and there was nothing in my room aside from Optimus Prime staring at me from atop of my Matchbox Car case. There was also the hint of a solitary cricket outside as if it continued from my dream. I laid back down and did my best to fall asleep for a few hours.

When I returned to school the next morning, I picked up my pencil to write, and something was different. I was able to close my hands a little bit and grip the pencil better. I said to myself, "Hmmmm, that's weird," and looked down at my hands. The cracking and bleeding weren't there, and the skin looked different. For the next three days, my hands improved to the point where there were still some raised bumps, but dramatically flattened, with no sandpaper texture anymore.

A week had passed, and it was time for my procedure. When I went to the doctor, the painful warts and deformities were all but gone. The doctor was astonished and called in his colleagues to take a look. None of them could believe the drastic change from only a few weeks prior. You could tell that my hands were still healing and not 100% perfect, but the doctor said, "We should wait and see what happens." I left the office, never returning. Within a few weeks, almost 6 years of pain and torture, simply looked like it never happened.

The physical healing was complete, but the kids at school didn't let me forget about my hands. I would always be the "kid with the warts" to them, no matter if they were gone or not.

Chapter 3:
The Apple & The Tree

While I had a good relationship with my Papa Lou-Lou, I've always felt a stronger connection to my dad's side of the family overall. I was named after my grandpa, Ben, who passed away several years before I was born at the age of 59. He died suddenly of a heart attack, leaving my grandma, Harriet, a widow until she passed away from cancer in the mid 1990s.

They were from Far Rockaway, which is how I wound up being born there in one of the local hospitals. There was always a connection to Rockaway as my grandma lived there until moving down to Florida. My father also finished up his career there. He kept a close eye on my grandma as NYC in the 1980s was a very dangerous place.

Rockaway is where my connection to the ocean began. Grandma Harriet used to bring me to the beach all the time to swim, while my dad would take me to the back bay behind her house. We'd turn over stones in the mud to look for "piss clams", fiddler crabs, and watch the bunker slap on the water when being chased by bluefish. There was also nothing like watching the sunset across Jamaica Bay. The orange light from the sun would mix with the haze and pollution of New York City, making the sky look like fluorescent cotton candy.

I'd stay over my grandma's house a lot when I was young and she taught me a lot about cooking and baking. By the age of 8, I was able to make my own breakfast, toast bagels, brownies from scratch, rugelach, lemon meringue pie, chicken soup, and pot roast. My parents never let me touch the oven at home, but grandma gave me free reign with her guidance.

Her and I had a special bond. There was nothing better than staying there and falling asleep to our favorite TV shows. She would even take me to see my dad on his foot post to say "hi" and get a moment of time with him. Rolling up in her rusted blue Buick and the Bee Gees playing on the mono speaker, she'd hum to the sound of the music. My dad and I would have some small talk before it was time for him to resume patrol.

While seeing my dad on post was fun, there was a specific moment when I realized the impact of him being an NYPD cop. It was during first grade in the month of October 1982; amidst all the chaos I had to deal with physically and emotionally as a young child. In fact, what was a definitive and dangerous moment in my dad's career, turned out to be a pivotal moment for me.

My dad was walking up the stairs of the 101st Precinct in Far Rockaway to sign out for the day, when he heard gunshots across the street from the Chemical Bank. Inside, two officers were involved in a standoff with two armed robbers. The next morning, an iconic photo graced one of the newspapers. It was my dad behind an RMP (patrol car) with his hat turned backwards; stretched across the hood of the car with his .38 revolver pointed at the bank.

Instantly, he became my hero and a topic of discussion at school. It was an escape for a moment. Kids wanted to talk to me regardless of how deformed my hands were. They were all curious about my dad, and what it was like for me to have him as my father. The teacher even invited him to talk to the class.

THE APPLE & THE TREE

I'll never forget the day he showed up to school. You could hear him walking down the granite and tile hallway as the sound of creaking leather, loud footsteps, and cuff keys jingling, interrupted the hushed environment. He was 5'11" on a good day, but he looked like a giant when he showed up to the door of the classroom.

The kids "oooh'd" and "ahhh'd" looking up at him while sitting on the floor. They patiently waited for him to speak through his grand mustache rivaling some of the most famous actors. He passed out NYPD-themed coloring books, told stories that made our teacher squirm uncomfortably in her seat, and had all the kids laughing and smiling.

It was a great day in my life and still is, even if not for another pivotal moment. When my dad was about to leave, the teacher said I could walk into the hallway and say goodbye to him. "Thank you, Dad," I said as I wrapped my arms around him with a big smile on my face. "I love you, Ben. I'll see you later," he replied.

My dad got up and began to walk away, but there was one more thing I had to say before he left. "Dad!" I yelled. He turned around and I said, "I wanna be a cop when I grow up." He walked back to me, got down on one knee, looked me straight in the eyes, and said, "I'll break your legs if you become a cop." My mouth was agape, and I ran back into the classroom as he walked away.

He wasn't joking. My dad didn't want me to do it and was always vocal about that. Whatever he went through on the job, he didn't want me to experience it. That moment was so impactful, for a long time it had me thinking about other careers and directions. However, there was always a dimly lit ember inside of me which could never be extinguished.

How could it not? Even after saying he'd "break my legs" if I wanted to be a cop, my dad still pointed out all the suspicious activity he saw as we drove around town to go to grandma's. He would always instill messages in me as far as staying away from certain situations, people, and drugs. Without him even realizing it, he was my training officer as a young kid, showing me the ropes of a place he didn't want me to go.

He even taught me how to fight, using a blend of boxing, pressure points, jiu-jitsu, and fight-for-your-life dirty street tactics to survive. There wasn't much I could do with my hands the way they were, but these lessons stayed with me as I healed, and still faced trouble in school.

There were a lot of lessons my dad taught me during this period, both direct and indirect. Even at a young age, I was able to pick up and understand a lot of behaviors around me. In some ways, I wanted to be just like him. In other ways, I wanted to be very different.

My parents would fight a lot when I was a kid, and I could always pick up on the fact that something was "off" with the relationship between them. My dad was a hardworking man who loved us very much. I'm sure my mom loved us too in her own way, but there was a streak of cruelness, and the need for control. It always boggled my mind how an NYPD cop, my hero, would be able to run into gunfire, run into burning buildings without any gear, and chase down some of the most violent men on the planet; yet be afraid to stand up to certain types of behavior at home.

The situation made me very independent for someone my age. It was a way to protect myself and not become like them couple-wise or how I treat others. This resulted in me becoming a "black sheep" of sorts, since I did things my way. I started to face problems head-on instead of running away from them. This apple definitely fell from the Reiver tree, but over time, the wind pushed it away to become something of its own. Regardless, my dad played a crucial role when it came to helping me deal with what was to come.

Chapter 4: Woodland

Back in the day, there was no "middle school" where you attended from 6th to 8th grade. It was considered "junior high school" in the 1980s and was 7th through 9th. Me being 12 years old and starting 7th grade walking amongst 9th graders, I felt like a little kid stuck in the throes of 1988. The term "little kid" was an understatement, since I was still one of the smallest kids in school.

It was a double whammy for me. All the snobby kids followed me from Barnum Woods Elementary School to Woodland Junior High. They blended with strangers coming from other schools around East Meadow. On one hand, I had all the kids still hounding me over a physical disability which didn't exist anymore. On the other hand, I was surrounded by "burnouts" and "metal heads" who smoked cigarettes outside before school and during lunch. It was very intimidating, and an automatic banishment to the "loser" table for me in the cafeteria.

Things were also changing at home since my dad retired from the NYPD a year prior. He was no longer the action hero I imagined him to be, and more like the other dads with 9-5 office jobs. Regardless, it was nice having him home more. He was my refuge in such a turbulent time. There was one lesson I learned during this period of change for my dad. When you retire, you're still a cop, and it still runs through your veins.

For a long time, I was afraid to tell my dad that I was being bullied. I was ashamed that his only son, the son of a tough cop, was being abused without fighting back. My apprehensions were a blend of my fear of getting in trouble, fear of my own strength, and losing. I thought that if I fought back and lost, things would get even worse.

It all came to a head several months before my 13th birthday and Bar Mitzvah. Coming from a Jewish family, my parents made me attend Hebrew school on weeknights and weekends, which I hated. It wasn't my lack of faith or anything like that. It was the atmosphere of hypocrisy that fills many establishments as the one I attended. Even at my age, I was able to sense something wasn't right.

Most of the snobby kids that bullied me in elementary school, also attended the same Hebrew school. The instructors allowed the bullying to happen, and their message overall didn't resonate with me. They were allowing hate to happen within their classroom. It is something that I deeply rejected, and it made the bullying worse, because I was a threat to the instructors for questioning certain things.

One evening in my classroom, surrounded by drawings of doves, messages of peace, and the Ten Commandments on the wall, the other kids conspired to humiliate me in front of everyone. Before class started, they had a girl start a fight with me as they all made a circle and trapped me. She started kicking and punching me while the other kids cheered and laughed. Remembering what my dad taught me about not hitting girls, I did not strike back and did my best to block everything.

Regardless, I was humiliated as everyone laughed, saying that I got beat up by a girl. Then, one of my only friends joined in the free-for-all, pointing and yelling, "Ha! You got beat up by a girl!" In an instant, rage filled me, and I saw red. He could see it in my eyes, and he ran out of the classroom. Like a lion triggered by movement of their intended prey, I broke through the circle of kids and instinctively ran after him.

He ran into the school office, then into the Hebrew school principal's room. At that point, the rage was burning so deep, I didn't care. As he hid behind the principal, I reached for him, threw him onto the desk, and proceeded to pound on him until he cried. My parents were called to the school as I sat in a chair against a wood-paneled wall of the office.

I remember the anger on my dad's face when he walked in and looked at me. He grabbed me by my shirt, yanked me into the hallway, and started yelling. I broke down crying and told him what happened. He got silent, stood up, dusted me off, put his hand on my cheek, and wiped away the tears on my face with his thumb. He took my hand and said, "come with me," and we went back into the office.

The Hebrew school principal went to speak, and my dad immediately cut him off while asking, "Did you ask Ben what happened?!" The principal's face turned ghost white and began to stutter, "Nuh, nuh, no." Then with his balls shriveled up, he muttered, "Your son is out of Hebrew school and won't be Bar Mitzvah'd here." My dad looked at him and said, "Good! We don't need your corrupt school anymore!" Before we walked out, he turned around to the principal and said, "I have a message for all these shitty kids. My son will no longer be a victim. I'm teaching him how to box, and he will fight back if anyone tries anything again."

We left that evening and I felt like I had my real dad back; the dad that stood up for what was right, defeated bad guys, and ran into danger. It was like watching Clark Kent leap out of his suit to become Superman one more time. After that, we grew very close as he spent a lot of time with me every day. He taught me how to box for real since my hands were fully healed. He was no longer just a dad, he was my coach, and my trainer.

In the meantime, the rabbi of the synagogue had a conference to smooth things over. While I was no longer allowed in Hebrew school, they decided to allow me to get Bar Mitzvah'd there. I went there once a week to study with the rabbi privately and learned my lines for the service. On the day of the ceremony and in true Ben fashion, when the principal met me on stage to shake my hand, I walked past his outstretched hand and refused to shake it. The congregation gasped, but I sent a clear message regarding him allowing bullying.

That moment in June, rolling into the summer, was the beginning of a lot of changes for me. While some things remained the same, I was starting to stand up for myself. Friends came and went as my neighbor and first crush moved away. She was one of the only girls who hung out with me, and we had a lot of fun together. We'd look for frogs and turtles in her backyard, ride bikes together, and she never judged me. It was my first heartbreak, and I never told her I liked her.

The summer of 1989 was a quiet one without her, and my small circle of friends grew even smaller as my parents were looking for homes in Florida. They got cold feet, and we never moved. However, just the rumor alone that we were moving, caused the few friends I did have, to distance themselves a little bit. 8th grade was waiting for me, and just like the month of March, it came in like a lion.

Woodland had a lot of tough kids. You wouldn't think so being out on Long Island, but a lot of these kids had experience fighting. Some came from abusive or broken homes, and some kids had tough fathers who were Korean or Vietnam War Veterans. East

Meadow is also the home to former UFC champion Matt Serra. While I never had to deal with him, there were others who were cut from the same cloth.

In 8th grade I was still one of the smallest kids in class and unfortunately, a new threat emerged. His name was Josh and for some reason, he picked me out of the crowd and started to torment me. While looking back and realizing he wasn't such a big guy, in relative terms, he was a giant to me back then. I may as well have been David and him, Goliath, since he lifted weights and probably outweighed me by 50+ pounds.

Every day, he'd follow me home, push me, spit on me, and do anything possible to get me to fight. While my dad was teaching me how to defend myself, part of me was still scared. I was still concerned about getting in trouble, hurt, or lose horribly and be tortured for the rest of my life. It came to the point where I'd come home every day and cry because I felt helpless.

One day I came home upset and my dad happened to be off from work. I told him what was going on and he said sternly, "What have I been teaching you for the past few months?" I began to sob, and with anger in his voice he said, "You need to stand up for yourself or this will haunt you forever!" I tried to fight back the tears saying, "What if I get hurt or get in trouble?"

I'll never forget these words when he said, "If you get into a fight, you go in expecting to get hurt, but I guarantee that win or lose, he will never bother you again if you make it inconvenient enough for him to fuck with you!" I whimpered and did a laughing snort at the same time as the NYC cop in him came out and he cursed. When I asked him about getting into trouble if I fight, he said, "As long as you don't start it, I have your back."

At that moment, a huge weight was lifted off my shoulders. It felt as if he was giving me permission to defend myself, even if I didn't need it. In my mind, it lifted away the fear of me disappointing him if I lost or got in trouble. The very next day, I was prepared to do battle, and it's a day I'll never forget.

I remember the blue skies, fast moving puffy clouds, and stiff breeze that graced the cool September day. I was walking home with a couple of friends, and Josh was back to do his thing. This time, his strategy to get me to fight was different. The conversation I had with my dad the day before, couldn't have come at a better time.

Josh came up from behind me and put me into a headlock, attacking me by surprise. This wasn't the typical pushing or name-calling; this was real. He was cutting off my air and everything started getting blurry. My friends were standing around doing nothing to help, but I could hear my dad's voice telling me, "Fight back, you have to fight back now!"

With all my strength, I wound my right hand back as far as I could; striking Josh in the lower spine with everything I had. He let go and grabbed his back, while I grabbed my hand in excruciating pain. My hand instantly broke as it hit his spine, and the damage I did to him was temporary compared to what I did to myself. Josh rushed in and tackled me as I was still gasping for air. The fight was over; he had me dead-to-rights.

He could've pounded me into oblivion, but hubris took over. Josh wanted to fight me standing up. Suddenly, he got up and waved his fists towards himself as if to stay, "Come on!" I got up, got my wits about me, and put my hands up. We began to circle on the lawn of someone's corner property. Cars drove by with their horns honking as a swarm of kids looked on.

Jab! His head snapped back. Jab! His head snapped back again. His eyes got as big as saucer plates, and you could see he didn't know what to do. I looked at my own hands in surprise that everything my dad taught me was there and it's working. Josh then threw a wild swing that I easily ducked and countered with another jab. His mouth started to trickle blood, and his face was bright red with fear and embarrassment.

He took one more swing in desperation. Forgetting my hand was broken for a second, I rolled under his feeble attempt, hitting him as hard as I could with a right hook. I almost knocked him down, while grabbing my hand in utter pain again. Josh was bent over as he looked down towards the ground. Blood from his mouth and nose dripped onto the sidewalk. He was broken and defeated.

"Finish him!" one of my friends yelled. I couldn't, I had nothing left. For a second, looking at him bent over and bleeding, I felt sorry for him. It didn't matter anyway. I was in so much pain that I couldn't finish him off even if I wanted to. I turned to my friend and said, "No, it's over. He's done," but I was done, too.

I ran home and the delayed adrenaline took over, alleviating the pain in my hand temporarily. As soon as I got in, I called my dad at his office and told him what happened. He said, "That's great! How do you feel?" "I feel great, dad!" I replied, "But I think my hand is broken." I looked down at my pulsating hand, and it was about the size of a purple-colored grapefruit.

The next 6 hours were spent at Nassau County Medical Center, where they put my broken hand back together, and placed a cast on it. My parents kept me home from school the next day to let the dust settle. That afternoon, the phone rang, and it was Josh calling to apologize. His parents made him call me after he was honest about what happened.

"You're a good fighter and could probably beat some of the toughest kids in school," I remember him telling me. I dismissed what he said, because to me, it was over. Deep inside, though, I knew I had a hidden talent even if I didn't have the size to back it up yet. Regardless, my fighting days were over I thought. The bully had been defeated and now everyone will leave me alone, but I couldn't be any more wrong.

Chapter 5: Peace Through Strength

After my fight with Josh and sending a clear message to anyone else looking to mess with me, I enjoyed a brief period of being a "celebrity" amongst the kids who used to tease me and treat me poorly back in elementary school. They had long forgotten about the kid with the warts and girls had no problem coming up to talk to me. I still had a small circle of friends and remained at the "loser" table during lunch, but it was more because they were loyal to me when times were bad. Things were changing for sure, although the storm clouds were gathering on another front.

With East Meadow being filled with a lot of tough kids, I now became the target of a test for them. The snobby kids weren't a threat to me ever again, but the "burnouts" and "metal heads" took notice. While I continued to hone my boxing skills with my dad as a trainer, I was still on the small side and didn't look like I could back up the stories circulating around. To them, I looked like low hanging fruit; a chance to look tough in other kid's eyes by beating a good fighter. Over the next 6 months, I went through a series of challenges that would alter the course of my life forever.

The first attempt by them was to try and goad me into a fight while I still had the cast on my right hand. The break I had was a bad one, and I had the cast for nearly 6 months. I was told by teachers that by the time I had the cast removed, I'd write just as well with my left hand as my right, but they were wrong. Just before the cast was removed, my handwriting was as bad as the first day. It looked like I was using my left foot to write. My left hand was good for one thing only, fighting.

I was walking down the hallway to put my books away, and one of the smaller burnouts came up to me and teased me about the cast on my arm; telling me I really lost the fight because I broke my hand. I knew it was a tactic to try and get me to fight, so I ignored him. He wouldn't let it go, and he shoved me when I turned my back to him to unlock my locker. My head hit the metal row of lockers. Although it didn't really hurt that bad, I turned around and hit him with a fierce left jab, knocking him down.

I picked him up by his hair and proceeded to punch him repeatedly with my one good hand until he was curled up in a ball, begging me to stop. A teacher came in between us and broke it up, and off to the principal's office we went. My dad had to come to school and pick me up, and they informed him that I was suspended for a day. He knew I didn't start it, so I didn't get in trouble. In fact, he took me to a Met game at Shea Stadium the very next day and didn't say a word to me.

I believe at that very moment, a monster of sorts was created. My dad was true to his word that he had my back if I didn't start a fight. However, taking me to the Met game also failed to teach me how to walk away. I took it as permission to use my talent to do whatever I wanted, as long as I wasn't the one starting trouble. When I returned to school the following week, the challengers started lining up to take me down, and one-by-one I faced them.

The first one was simple and fast, with nobody getting in trouble. He was a tall kid with blonde hair and always wore the same Guns N' Roses t-shirt to school. They loved to try and get me at my locker. I was at my most vulnerable since my back was turned and my hands were full. He grabbed my lunch and held it high above his head, taking advantage of his height and my lack of any. I turned around, jumped up, and tried to grab it, but he kept bringing it up higher and teasing me.

I began to get so angry, I couldn't hear what he was saying anymore. All I could see was him smiling and laughing at me. With his left hand at his side and his right hand held up high with my lunch bag, I hit him with an uppercut, knocking him down. I picked up my lunch off the floor and walked away. I never heard from him again and he stayed far away from me. However, the problems kept piling up.

The next kid was very tough, and it's the only fight I ever lost in the street. He was a big kid, and I still didn't really have the strength to back up the skill. Nothing I threw at this kid hurt him and he just kept coming. Unlike that bully Josh, when he tackled me to the ground, this one didn't let me go. While it wasn't that bad in hindsight, it was the worst beating I took at the time. He was too heavy to get off me, and I just did my best to block his punches that crashed through my defense. Even in defeat, he left me alone. Nobody knew much about that fight because it wasn't in school. It happened only a few blocks from my house in front of a small handful of kids, so he didn't get any "credit" for it at school, and kids still wanted a piece of me.

The final matchup was with this kid, Henry, who was 16 years old and still in 8th grade. As with the other burnouts at the time, he loved his heavy metal T-shirts and smoked cigarettes all day. He was a fighter and had the reputation of giving other kids bloody noses in the hallway. You could tell that he was on another level and mentally disturbed; possibly coming from a broken or abusive home.

It didn't matter. There was no level of empathy for him that would stop his terror. He was in my home-economics class and zeroed in on me after the other fights I got into. He'd just stare at me all period, not saying a word. For those who understand the Charles Manson look, he had "it" in his eyes.

One day in class, he decided to use the giant gap in his teeth to launch a long stream of spit at me from a few feet away. He did this several times and I told him to stop. It happened again, and I stood up and told him to stop loud enough for the teacher to hear. He stood up too, and spit in my face again. In the middle of the classroom, I hit him with a straight right hand. His head snapped back and returned to its normal position. He sneered at me, saying, "You're dead!"

I hit him again and he just looked at me, then we started to wrestle. There is a huge difference between a 13-year-old and a 16-year-old as far as strength, and it was obvious. He backed me up against the radiator on the wall, hit me with a headbutt, then punched me on the right side of my neck with a left hook. The teacher was screaming at us to stop. I was holding his arms so he couldn't hit me, but he kept trying to ram his head forward and hit me again. I couldn't believe how strong he was.

The door to the classroom burst open, and it was the principal coming to try and break us up. I thought to myself, "I need to get a good shot in before this ends," so I let go of his left arm with my right hand and snuck in a short uppercut. He finally went down, looked at me with his crazed eyes, and tried to get up. Before he could, the principal was on him, throwing him across the classroom like a rag doll.

The craziest thing of all is that they never separated us and let things cool down. Instead of giving us home suspension like the other fight earlier in the school year, the principal gave us 5 days of in-school suspension. It was in an isolated room, sitting right next to one another, and unsupervised.

Every day, I'd stare forward and do my work, while Henry was a foot away from my right ear, saying, "You're dead, you're dead, you're dead," repeatedly. It got to the point where I couldn't take it anymore and we brawled briefly again in the suspension room. He was like the monster in a horror movie and kept getting up, even after I picked up a desk and slammed it down over him.

Just after my 14th birthday, we had one final fight on a hot day in June before school ended. It was inside of a dried-out water basin a few blocks from the school. We walked alone to the gated off area after dismissal. Not saying a word to each other, we climbed through a small hole in the fence, trekked down the weed-covered hill, and onto the dry, hot sand. It was like a scene out of an old western movie; just him and I, waiting for the other to make a move.

It felt like an eternity, but it was maybe a minute or two before we both moved in on each other. I threw my signature jab and he ducked, hitting me with a left hook. I went down to one knee, which was the last time I was ever down in my life. "I'm gonna kill you!" he said as he looked at me with his "Manson" eyes. I believed him. He was there to finish business. It was then when I remembered some of those fight-for-your-life dirty tactics my dad taught me.

The "rules" were out of the window. I was fighting for something different, something I didn't encounter again until being in uniform 17 years later. If I didn't win, he was going to kill me and leave me there laying in the sandpit. As he approached slowly to finish me off, I grabbed a fistful of sand and threw it in his face. It wasn't like in the movies where someone is blinded, but it was enough for me to pop back up and rush at him. I came up from behind him, put him in a headlock, and squeezed as tight as I could. Even with his face turning purple, I didn't care. The fear of him killing me, made me want to kill *him*. It was as primal as it gets, and I held on until he dropped unconscious. I took a step back, out of breath, watching him motionless on the sand. I thought for a second that I killed him, but I saw his abdomen moving up and down. I left him there on the hot sand, and I climbed out of the water basin a different person; a killer, even if I had not killed him.

It was the end of life as I knew it at the time. My parents were scared for me, and some of my friends were scared *of* me. All the kids that treated me poorly and now treated me right, distanced themselves from me in fear. I was a different person to them after all those fights. I became perceived as the bully and the one who uses his hands too fast. However, I was still the same Ben inside and just wanted to be left alone. That year, Woodland became a middle school that was only 7th and 8th grade. This meant in late June of 1990, we graduated with the 9th graders, and we were all heading to East Meadow High School; everyone except for me. It was decided by the school district and my parents that I needed a change of scenery. They were tired of me getting into fights, even if I didn't start them.

That fall, I was sent to W.T. Clarke High School in Westbury to start a new life with kids I didn't know. By standing up for myself, I solved one issue and created another by being "sent away". Looking back, it was still the right thing to do, and I would do it all over again. Had I not stood up for myself, where would I be right now? My path was slowly solidifying like a concrete and steel foundation.

Chapter 6: Intermezzo

The summer before going into high school and high school itself, could be considered a "palate cleanser" of sorts. It was a relatively easy time in my life compared to anything prior. Instead of needing several drams of over-proofed whiskey to talk about infancy through my first year as a teenager, this would require a nice glass of rum. Yes, it had the typical challenges of a teenager, but looking back it was a lot of fun.

I went from being ostracized and finding the fighter in me, to having my first kiss and first girlfriend at Camp Coleman in Freeport, NY. It's where a lot of families on the south shore of Long Island sent their kids, and it was my first "job" as a message runner at their headquarters. It was nice because I had free reign of the camp, and my girlfriend and I would sneak away to steal a kiss whenever we could. Like most summer romances, we never made it into autumn, but we always kept in touch long after camp.

As far as fighting, the only fight I got into was with a miniature ram at the nature shack. I was helping other workers feed the animals, and it rammed me with its horns square in my back. To this day I can still re-live the stinging pain across my spine, and I have yet to return to a petting zoo if anything has horns in the pen. I also can't stand alpacas, but that's for another book.

Heading into 9th grade, I felt "prepared" having my first kiss and no longer nervous about girls. I also had a new cast on my hand, which happened when I punched a wall in frustration after my mom played one of her head-games. A "boxer's fracture" they called it, although it had nothing to do with boxing. Being the new kid in school, having a cast, and coming to Clarke with a reputation from East Meadow, allowed me some good attention.

Not only did everyone leave me alone for the most part, but some of the girls took a liking to me as well. One girl in social studies used to send me notes written in French. To this day I have no clue what it said, but she'd always smile at me and blush. There was only one girl who had my attention. She was a petite nerdy girl with braces. I knew she had potential, but I had to find a way into the nerdy circle of kids since my grades wouldn't "qualify".

I wound up having a wide range of friends and didn't belong to any one group. Clarke was much different than East Meadow since kids got along better with each other. Because of this, I found myself invited to one of the nerdy kid's birthday parties. Still being somewhat new, I felt as if I were a scientist researching the behavior of an unknown species; living amongst them as they cautiously learned about me, too.

In a moment that I hoped for, in came the girl I watched walk the halls for the past month. Occasionally, I would catch her looking down the hall at me, but I wasn't sure if she liked me or not. Despite the fact that I was hoping she'd be at the party, I was suddenly a nervous kid again with her in the same room. To my advantage, a couple of friends knew I liked her. Unbeknownst to me, our friends were scheming to force us to interact with each other through a game of "truth or dare".

Word travels fast in high school and by the following week, the "cool" kids were busting my chops about liking her. They kept asking me, "Why her?" making fun of the way she looked and

INTERMEZZO

saying that I would get caught on her braces if we tried to kiss. After having gone what I went through when I was younger, I knew what it was like to be ostracized. I chose to ignore everyone, and she wound up being my first "true" girlfriend.

Not long after we started dating, it was time for her braces to come off. I can recall the moment like it was yesterday. I went to pick her up for a school dance that night, and in a surprise move, her braces were gone. She looked like an angel walking down the steps in her white dress, white gloves, and gleaming white smile. Our parents said the look on my face was priceless. I felt like a king that night and now all the cool kids wanted what I had in my arms.

Eventually, one of them got what they wanted, and she started dating a giant football player after we broke up in 10th grade. It was a painful breakup, but in the end, it was no fault but my own. Being the new kid in school and having a completely different life compared to just a year prior, got to my head. The nerdy girl with braces became a cheerleader, the new guy "shtick" wore off, and such is the circle of life. It sounds sad, but the lesson here is not one of loss. I had given a girl with braces a chance, and in return, she gave me a chance. Her parents also treated me as if I were family, and I had a great time while it lasted.

Even though in retrospect things weren't that bad, I got into a real funk and withdrew from having such a large group of friends. I essentially became a wallflower, having a very small social circle. My style of clothing changed, too. I went from being "stylish" and looking like the lost member of a boy band, to a simple t-shirt and jeans kind of guy. I focused on the things that I loved, which was art and boxing. Obviously, those are two very contrasting things, but boxing in the gym kept me from wanting to fight anyone who crossed my path in a bad way. Knowing I could fight well, was good enough for me. For the rare time I had a problem, I'd just let them run their mouths and walk away.

Art class was my favorite subject in school, regardless of the love I had for science and social studies. It allowed me to do the things I couldn't do when my hands were disabled as a kid. I also had some great friends in art, and we had a lot of laughs. One of the funniest moments of my life, was when the class worked with pastels.

My friend Tony, with whom I'm still friends with today and creator of this book cover, was a very talented artist even back then. He was very dedicated to his work, and I was very unserious about mine. Our two personalities clashed in what became a decades-long battle over a missing portrait.

To this day I can't remember what I even made. Tony's work overshadowed mine and all the current events going on around the world at the time. Like a gift from the tan gods, Tony's hand was guided to make a very lifelike and very hysterical portrait of wrestler, Hulk Hogan. Every day I walked by his work in progress, I would start laughing to his chagrin.

Who couldn't find this thing funny? It was so tan, so angry, and so lifelike at the time. Its eyes would follow you around the room. All you can hear in your head was Hulk Hogan saying, "Whatcha gonna do!" and I'd start laughing all over again. When the project was finished, the teacher had us put our work on top of the cabinet for display. I still remember exactly where Hogan was in the room, and I remember when he went missing.

I asked Tony, "Where did Pastel Hogan go?" Like a mobster out of a gangster movie, he said, "It's gone," and he walked away calmly. I asked him for months where it was, but he was legitimately upset with me that I always laughed at it, and he refused to bring it back. For the next 2 years, there was a space

INTERMEZZO

missing on top of the cabinets where Pastel Hogan used to be, and a hole in my heart.

When we reconnected on social media years later, one of the first things I asked was, "Do you still have Pastel Hogan?" The fuse was lit again, and he vehemently denied its existence, but I knew he was lying. I created online petitions, poems, funny posts, anything to make Tony break, but he wouldn't budge. Eventually one day he tagged me in a post, and it was a photo of the tan anomaly. "I knew he was alive!" I said to Tony. It was as if there was peace in this world again, and the Ark of the Covenant was returned to its rightful place. Friends gathered around me, friends that didn't even know Tony growing up, to marvel at the tan and sweat created from simple chalk sticks.

Throughout the fun and laughs, I was still pre-occupied with my broken heart. Every day I had to see my ex-girlfriend walk down the halls with her Cro-Magnon teen boyfriend. It was during this time that I had my first experience with a special ability that would save my life and the lives of others. However, not before there was a major lesson to be learned. I forgot exactly what happened one night and why, but I remember crying myself to sleep.

"She still loves you," a voice was heard as I was shaken out of my sleep. I looked around and there was nothing but darkness. I knew it was a dream, but it didn't feel like one. "She still loves you, but you have to move on," the calm, soothing voice said. "Who are you?" I asked while pulled into a blinding white light and no ground below me. "I am Ben," he said. "What do you want?" I replied with confusion and fear in my voice. "You know why I'm here," he said very sternly.

The light went black as if I was sucked out of a vacuum and jolted awake. I had no idea what just happened, but it felt so real. I never met my Grandpa Ben, but it was so familiar. I knew it was him. I knew what he looked like, sounded like, and his personality. He came to try and help me at my lowest point, but all I could hear in my teenage mind was that she still loved me, and not the moving-on part.

The following evening, I called my ex-girlfriend and told her what happened. I begged her to tell me if it was true or not, and she tearfully admitted that she still loved me. It was one of the worst things I could ever do to someone. At that very moment, the vision of my grandpa and his message were validated. I also tried to use it to my advantage and get my ex-girlfriend back, but it backfired. The pain and fear I caused, made her run further away from me, and deeper into her boyfriend's arms.

I went against the Universe, and it kicked my ass worse than any opponent ever could. It made me retreat into myself more, and I became the shy and nervous kid I was long ago. Because of my lack of confidence, I found myself in the "Friend Zone" with a few girls throughout this period. It was a comfortable place for me. I didn't have to worry about rejection even if I liked some of them. A lot of my friends still poke fun at me about the friend zone back then and all the stories that came from it, but for the most part, it was a choice on my behalf.

In the meantime, my mind was pleasantly distracted by a new addition to our family. My dad decided to get a boat so that we could spend time together. He figured it would be nice to do some fishing, without being elbow-to-elbow on a crowded party boat. It was a great time for us as we spent the weekends cleaning, restoring, and outfitting this beat-up-looking boat from the 1970s. Regardless, we made it our own, and restored it back to its original tri-hull ugliness that served us well until into the early 2000s.

It was here where I cut my teeth on the south shore waters of Long Island and New York City; learning seamanship and where to catch the most fish. One day, we even took our 18ft jalopy 10 miles offshore to an area called the "Angler Bank" in search of big fluke (summer Flounder). A big sport fishing boat drifted by and the captain yelled at us (for being so far offshore), "Hey! You're really nuts!" and the name of the boat was born. I spent the next week carefully placing stenciled letters on the side of the boat, making sure it was perfectly level with the chalky-blue fiberglass stripe which ran down the side. "Reel Nuts" was her name and we enjoyed every minute of it.

The experience gave me enough of a base to start seeking paid work on other boats as my love grew for the ocean and hard physical work. It was also very lucrative for a kid my age. As time went on, I began to build up enough hours towards my captain's license, but I was way too young at the time to go through with it. I continued to learn about the sea and taking the boat out into storms on purpose without my dad's consent. I wanted to learn every aspect that the ocean had to offer, even if it were dangerous. It was a calling for me and I was addicted to the freedom.

Being on the water alone at 16 years old also afforded me a lot of time to think and examine my life. I knew I had to make some changes but didn't know how. When I was out there alone, I found myself whispering to the ocean and asking it questions. I also knew my Grandpa Ben loved the ocean as much as my dad and I did. It offered me a connection to him despite not visiting me again until I was much older.

Eventually, I listened to my grandfather's advice from that fateful night and wound up moving on with the help of a chance encounter at another party. It was at a Sweet 16 where I was forced to hold hands with a girl. We all gathered around and danced to the song, "That's What Friends Are For" at the end of the party. It was your typical cheesy ending for any Long Island extravaganza. After that cold winter night during 11th grade, she would smile at me whenever we saw each other in the hallway at school.

I was too shy, and our friends knew it, so a mutual friend of ours spoke to her after asking me if I liked her. We went on a date to the local movie theater, and the rest was history. She wound up becoming my "high school sweetheart" as we dated on and off throughout college and young adulthood. I had a "type", and she wasn't it with her blonde hair and relatively tall stature. I walked down the hallway like a king once again, with one of the best-looking girls in school at my side. She also became a cheerleader like my ex, but this time nobody would steal my girlfriend. Only the path I was about to take, was enough to push us away from one another.

PART II

Chapter 7: Master of None

Many individuals who are good at a lot of things, but not great at one particular thing, have a hard time deciding what to do in life. I fell into that category as I enjoyed so many things and had a lot of talents. I was going to school originally with the intent of becoming a meteorologist due to my love for science. My birthday was a notorious time for severe thunderstorms in the Northeast, and it always captivated me. At the same time, my love for boxing and dedication to it, proved to be a distraction when it came to school.

It was a confusing time for me when others already had things figured out. I was juggling boxing, boating, school, artistry, photography, and writing, all at once. It was too much and caused me to burn the candle at both ends when you also factor in my girlfriend. She had decided to stay home from college to be with me, studying locally instead of going out-of-state. It was a big point of contention, and she felt pressured by me to stay home for someone "going nowhere".

I was also putting myself through school and working full time at the local P.C. Richard & Son. They were a well-known electronics store across Long Island and New York City. How I kept up with it all, while working on a fishing boat too, is beyond me. I certainly couldn't do that much now being middle-aged, but I continued to push forward despite trying to handle too many activities.

Working for the electronics store was a lot of fun and I met a lot of people; some of whom remain my friends to this day. We worked hard, played hard, and made a decent amount of money for young adults our age. I was good at what I did and with little effort. I didn't need to be a pushy, stereotypical salesman, and naturally got along with customers.

Some of my regular customers were celebrities. They consisted of professional hockey players, football players, singers, and rap artists. I even had a former NYPD police commissioner as a customer and half-owner of the NY Mets, Nelson Doubleday Jr. Even with all the cool stories and experiences, my girlfriend hated what I did for work. She was embarrassed to tell people about my job. There was a stigma in her mind about being a salesman, even if I wasn't going to make a career out of it.

To me, I was enjoying life and pursuing the things I thought had promise. I was good at what I did boxing-wise and had all the tools my dad did in the ring. Because of the way I was taught, I was an old-school fighter. I had heavy hands, a good chin, and speed to match. The only problem I encountered was height and build. At 5'9" and 168lbs, many of the fighters in my weight class were taller. I couldn't lose much more weight due to my heavy legs, but that's where I generated my power.

I was exciting to watch, and a local promoter I knew from work, took notice. We got to know each other, and he invited me to work a couple of his fights on Long Island. I oversaw security for the ring girls, and I also had to make sure some of the fighters behaved. It was bizarre to see the inner workings of the industry. Boxing was a very dirty business, but I ignored it all to try and get an opportunity down the road.

MASTER OF NONE

On a summer night in July at the age of 20, I was driving home from my girlfriend's house in my beat-up 1990 Ford Escort. The windows were open, and I was enjoying some music. The stereo system I had was probably worth about 3 times as much as the car itself. One of my favorite songs, "Make Me Lose Control" by Eric Carmen came on. I was 12 years old when the song came out, and it was the first song I ever danced to with a girl.

Driving along without a care in this world, the music volume dropped on its own. It was an analog volume knob, so I'm not sure how that happened. I twisted the volume knob up again, and it went back down. I went to turn it up again in frustration, and the stereo turned off. "Put your seatbelt on!" a gruff voice barked in my ear. It was as if someone was sitting next to me, but nobody was there. The Ford Escort at the time had automatic seatbelts with a separate lap belt I had to put on manually. Out of laziness I never wore it before, but like a kid getting scolded by a parent, the voice prompted me to put it on.

About 15 seconds later, a car went head-on with me in an offset crash in the intersection. I had about 1 second to react, turning the wheel just enough where it crushed the passenger side of the hood instead of mine. Regardless, the impact was severe. My head hit the steering wheel with such force that it knocked me out. When I came to, everything hurt. All I could hear was ringing in my ears. My vision was blurry to the point where I could hardly see. Blood trickled down the side of my face, my nose, and my mouth.

I don't remember much after that, but once again, my life veered off the tracks and shifted my path once again. I was out of work for quite some time, out of school for 2+ years, and the boxing dream was dead. I was lucky to be alive, though. If it weren't for the mysterious voice telling me to put my lap belt on, I'd be dead for sure. However, the lap belt did a job on me despite the fact that it kept me alive. In the summer of 1998, it was discovered that I had an injury doctors missed, and it required surgery.

Just before getting the news about needing surgery, I was in the process of starting school again. Due to the severe concussion from hitting the steering wheel, I had to adjust for my abilities since I had lost a lot of my math skills. I didn't care at this point. It was all about getting a diploma for the sake of my girlfriend as she became more impatient with me.

Up until this moment, I had no thoughts of becoming a cop since that pivotal scene in first grade with my dad, but something happened during the accident. At the scene, a witness told the officer they overheard the driver saying that it's a good thing the cop didn't know they just came from a bar. They alerted the officer, but he didn't take any action and ignored the witness. It haunted me for a long time, and I always said to myself that I'd never do that to a victim if I were a cop.

The surgery was set for the week after my sister's wedding, and it was deemed a success. About 2 weeks later, I wound up having an infection where the incision was. It was a dangerous infection, and they gave me an antibiotic that almost destroyed my entire body. Weeks after taking the pills, I was playing baseball with a few friends. I began to suffer from weird muscle spasms in my legs. Throughout the next few weeks, it ate away at my muscles, tendons, and ligaments.

I could barely move or pick anything up. Even something simple as lifting a VCR box at work, made it feel as if the muscles were going to rip off my bones. It took me nearly 2 more years to recover from that. It required intense physical therapy, steroids, and special diets to keep me from getting violently ill. My body as I knew it changed completely. I looked different, felt different, and was now prone to injury. That little ember glowing in me again to be a cop, was extinguished by the likelihood I'd never be able to get through a police academy without getting hurt.

The entire episode from accident to surgery, to illness and being temporarily disabled, became a catalyst for something I only had glimpses of up until that point in my life. Green lights, visitation dreams, and disembodied voices, all with a purpose to help me, started to become more familiar, and more frequent. The voice in the car which saved my life, was a wakeup call that something was going on, and that my life had direction for a purpose. Whatever was happening, it felt as if I were being prepared for something as I healed from everything.

One night I was in bed, and I couldn't fall asleep. Tossing and turning, I decided to lay on my back and close my eyes, even if I couldn't sleep. I tried to think of anything that was relaxing, and in almost an instant, I was in somebody's car. I wound up being in their front passenger seat, riding up Glen Cove Road in Carle Place, NY. I was watching the person drive, but they couldn't see me. It was an old man driving late at night. He was wearing a wool hat and looked like Mark Twain with his grey mustache.

As his car passed under the railroad bridge by Jericho Turnpike, my body was sucked out of the car and into a speeding train heading towards New York City. I was then sitting on the plastic seats in an empty train, all alone with a sense of calmness about me. I was just a passenger along for the ride. My girlfriend's house at the time was near the train tracks in New Hyde Park. As we passed her house, I was transferred to her bedroom. The only thing that lit up the room was her alarm clock, and I was able to read the time that displayed 2:03am.

I watched my girlfriend sleep with her cat curled up at the end of the bed. When I kneeled to touch her face, the cat woke up, started purring, and crawled over. The cat was able to see me somehow. I smiled and went to pet her, but she leapt back and hissed in fear. I glanced at the clock quickly and it read 2:06am, then I was immediately back in my bed at home. For the rest of the night, I didn't sleep due to a fierce headache and wondering what just happened.

The next day, my girlfriend and I saw each other. She told me she didn't sleep well because her cat woke her up around 2am. "She jumped and began hissing," she said, "But there was nothing there." I told her about what happened to me, and she freaked out. I'm not sure to this day if she believed me, but things kept happening and began to put a strain on our relationship.

My mind began thinking "ahead" and seeing all sorts of paths. A "gut feeling" on steroids is the only way I can describe it. "Do this," "Don't do that," all kinds of advice started flowing in, and I was seeing things and hearing voices. These were not visual or auditory hallucinations. It was something else, something cosmic. Whatever it was, I was in tune with it. I even applied it at work, reading my customers better, and making more money than I ever did.

The other salespeople couldn't understand what was going on. Because of school, I was working 34 hours a week compared to their 60 hours, but I was making a lot more money than they were. People I didn't know were coming in, walking right past the other guys, and asking for me. It felt as if I were in a video game and had the "cheat" codes to breeze through every challenge.

This newfound ability and sudden change in my quality of life, also had a negative impact. Things with my girlfriend began to deteriorate after we moved in with each other. I was in this world, focused on work, and my mind was essentially on another planet. In her mind, I was *still* going nowhere, and far away from finishing school. She became obsessed with me getting a degree, but I wasn't as worried about it as she was.

We were on different planes of consciousness, and I began to submit myself to whatever journey I was on. According to her, I was lazy and unfocused, because I wasn't pursuing the things she wanted of me. It was more about her. She felt that if I wasn't doing what she wanted, we couldn't get married and start a family. The relationship became broken, and two good people became very toxic towards each other. There was never any abuse, physical or otherwise, but we began to fight a lot, and our relationship became more distant.

Things began to unravel even more when we had an argument and wound up sleeping in separate bedrooms. I closed my eyes and went to sleep, and a voice in my head said, "You're a fighter, get back on that bag!" Then a warm green light enveloped me, taking me to a very small boxing gym. I was watching myself hitting a heavy bag, my arms getting tired, and I was dropping my hands. An old man was yelling at me, encouraging me to keep going. He looked familiar and I knew his face, but I couldn't figure out who he was.

The next morning, all I could do was think about boxing, even if my body was still broken and weak. I knew that if I started again, I'd get hurt, but it became a mission to seek out some answers as to why the green light took me there.

Chapter 8: Pillar to Post

During early 2000 and at almost 24 years old, I had begun to make some changes in my life. I stopped seeking the approval of others and became unfazed about what people thought about me. My decisions started taking a toll on the relationship with my parents as well as my girlfriend, but I didn't care. I felt as if I was going nowhere due to life-changing setbacks, and I needed to take control by following the messages given to me.

One of those messages came to me, when I decided to take the back roads to Roosevelt Field Mall in Garden City, NY. I always took the Meadowbrook Parkway to the mall exit, but this time I just felt like taking another route. As I crossed over the train tracks near the mall, I saw a sign that read, "Gleason's Boxing Gym: Open Here," with an arrow pointing down an industrial area behind the mall. Gleason's is a famous boxing gym in Brooklyn, NY. It is the home-place to many world champions and world-class trainers. Apparently, they decided to open a small "satellite" gym on Long Island.

"Gleason's Gym? What are they doing here?" I asked myself. Instead of going to the mall to get my girlfriend another trinket-of-apology, I chose to make a right turn down the road. The road itself was cratered and worn from all the neglect of heavy trucks going in and out. It was as if it were in a war zone hit with cluster bombs. I bounced down the road, nearly bottoming-out my college car, a Mazda Protege with over 100,000 miles on it.

I walked inside the small gym and there was an old man behind a tiny desk by the door. With a salty demeanor he asked, "Whaddya want, kid?" in his old-timey NY/Looney Tunes accent. "I'm not a kid," I huffed back at him. "Well? Whaddya here for?" he replied as if I were wasting his time. I let him know about my boxing experience and the accident. I told him I wanted to start all over again and return to the ring. "Well, you don't look like much of a boxer to me, but sure I'll take your money," he apathetically said with a half-smile. I gave him some cash and told him I'd be back the next day.

When I walked out and went back to the car, it hit me that he was the man in my vision the green light took me to. His name was Al Gavin, one of the most well-known cut men in the business. I raced home to tell my girlfriend what happened, and my excitement was met with skepticism. It was a long time since I went to a boxing gym or got in the ring, and she was afraid I'd get hurt. When I called my dad, I got the same treatment from him. They were hoping I'd listen to their concerns, but I didn't care and showed up at the gym the following day.

Dressed in sweatpants and sneakers, the other guys in the gym laughed at me. I was a rookie all over again and it showed. My arms were as thin as noodles, still recovering from when the antibiotics withered away my muscles. However, the heavy hands and mechanics were still there. Al was impressed with my power from the get-go, even if he hid it well. I laced up the gloves and started hitting the bag as Al sat in a steel folding chair, ignoring the goings-on of the gym.

Pop! I hit the bag and smiled to myself, knowing something was still there. Pop! Pop! Thud! The bag shook as I hit it with two jabs and a right hook. Al turned his chair around and started watching me. "Start movin' ya head!" he yelled. "If ya don't move ya head, you'll get killed!" he exclaimed. I started moving my head more, hitting the bag for another 15-20 minutes, but I started to tire out fast. It was already enough for me for that day, and I had a long way to go stamina-wise.

"Quittin' so soon?" Al asked while laughing. I turned to him full of sweat and said with my head hung low, "I gotta work on it." "No shit ya gotta work on it, see ya tomorrow....and start doing some roadwork!" he yelled as the door closed behind me. I walked down the hall and got back in my car. My clothes were soaked through with sweat and I was out of breath. I had a very long way to go, and this was just the beginning. My body had to be built back up again, and Al was the man to do it. I was brought there for a reason, and I wasn't about to quit.

With my face flushed from being out of breath and my muscles already seizing up as I drove home, I immediately went into a hot bath to relax as soon as I got in. I forgot the next morning that I had school and work, so I missed the next day at the gym. It was probably a blessing in disguise as I had to pop pain meds all day to move, but Al was pissed when I showed up again.

"I thought ya wanted to get back to form!" he barked at me when I showed up a few days later. "I do, but I forgot I had work and school," I said back. "Well come here before or after work and school," he said while throwing me a set of keys to let myself in. Now I had no excuse, and I felt like I had something to prove to him by not looking lazy. "Now hit that bag again until ya can't lift ya arms," saying as he walked back to his seat while turning his back to me. "Move that head!" he yelled again without even looking at me.

For the next few months, I began running again, hitting the heavy bag, and lifting weights to get my body stronger. I also had to relearn the speed bag because my coordination was gone. My body would never be the same again, so I had to build a different version of it. I would be heavier, stronger, but slower. There was no other choice. I wasn't slick anymore or had the same reaction time. I knew it and Al knew it too.

"Whaddya lookin' to do with this?" he came up to me and asked one day. I looked at a poster on the wall for the 2001 New York State Golden Gloves, and I said while pointing, "That." He looked at the poster, scoffed at me, and said with empathy for the first time, "You need a lot of work, kid. You're not close to being ready for something like that." "I know, but I don't care," I replied.

"Well, it's my job to care and my responsibility!" Al clapped back. "You don't understand, it's something I have to do. I don't know why, but I have to do it," I said while looking at him with a determined face. "Fine, kid, but it'll cost you," he said with his now infamous half-smile. "I'll work with you, but I don't do it for free," he continued. Making the money I made at P.C. Richard & Son, I was prepared to pay whatever money it took to follow through with the mission I was on. Al gladly took my money. He started working with me more and did so without turning his back to me in his steel chair.

One day we were in the gym, and I was having an off day physically. "You're a fighter, get back on that bag!" he yelled. I stopped and looked at him for a second. I was in shock from remembering the green light showing him and I working together, saying the exact same thing. "What?" he asked as I stopped hitting the bag, looking at him. "Nothing," I mumbled as I started hitting the bag again. I was so tired and could hardly lift my arms anymore. However, I kept going in order to try and "defeat" the green light depicting me as weak.

I spent that night not only popping pain meds again because my entire body felt like it was encased in a block of cement, but I also just stared at the ceiling. "Was this light guiding me towards my death?" I asked myself as I felt horrible physically. It was a long time until I began to understand the pattern going on and when something was trying to help. Whatever it was, it was keeping me from stopping, and I kept listening even though I didn't understand yet. My girlfriend slinked into bed and said to me, "Why don't you just quit?" With a tired voice I replied, "I can't," and drifted off to sleep.

After a one-week break and getting some rest, I returned to the gym and Al had given me a list of equipment to get. "What's this?" I asked. "You're sparring next week, and I don't want ya getting your teeth knocked out or ya balls busted in," he replied. I was excited to finally get back in the ring and that he deemed me worthy to do so. I rushed over to the local shop and got some new shorts, boxing shoes, mouthpiece, and groin protector. A few days later, I wound up receiving the worst beating of my life.

When I climbed into the ring, I immediately knew I was in trouble. Sparring isn't meant to go for the knockout, and my opponent didn't, but Al wanted the guy to go hard to send me a message. I wasn't ready, and he wanted me to know it. The bell rang and we met each other in the middle of the ring. Pop! He hit me with a jab. "Move ya head!" Al yelled. I threw a jab back and just missed, so I doubled-up on the next volley and landed one of the two.

He smiled at me and threw another jab of his own. Pop! My head snapped back again. Despite being able to take a good punch, it stung. "Move ya damn head!" Al yelled as he slammed his hands on the canvas. I threw a lead right hand to reply to the onslaught. He ducked and countered with his own punch, sending me into the corner. My opponent rushed in after me, hit me with a few body shots, and backed off as to not go for the knockout.

We did 3 rounds of this. Although I didn't quit and tried to fight back, he was younger, faster, and stronger. He beat me from pillar to post that evening, and it was the first time my nose bled from anything other than the car accident. "Good job, kid," Al said to me in a soft tone as I climbed out of the ring. Everything hurt, and I knew right then and there that I wasn't as good as I used to be. It had been over 4 years since I was in the ring, and I didn't feel like I should be in there anymore.

I went home that evening, got back in the tub, and wanted to cry. Everything hurt and it felt as if I had been in another car accident. It felt all wrong, and I questioned myself as to what I was doing. My friends, girlfriend, and family begged me to stop when they saw my face scuffed up and slightly swollen from the sparring match, but I couldn't quit. A few days later, I showed back up to the gym with my tail between my legs and still some marks on my face.

Al was shocked that I returned to the gym. I'm not sure if he was trying to test me or trying to get me to quit, but he was shocked, nonetheless. I walked in, didn't say a word, put my hand wraps on, laced up the gloves, set the timer, and started hitting the bag again. Pop! Pop! Thud! Pop! Thud! Thud! I hit the bag for 30 minutes with anger and determination. Al walked over and said to me, "Ya showed up today, that says something. Let's start again tomorrow." I nodded my head and kept going to the gym, getting back into the ring, and improving with each session.

As the weeks wore on, I was landing more shots, cutting the ring off more effectively, and not finding myself overwhelmed anymore. However, there were a few deficiencies, and Al took me aside to have an honest conversation. He told me that I had great power, a good chin, and good fundamentals, but he was concerned about my head movement and reaction time. "Ya got great power for your weight class, and I like how you cut off the ring and attack, but we need to be realistic about this," he said. "With your height, you should be in a lower weight class. If you don't win by knockout, you're gonna get out-pointed every time." I couldn't lose any more weight without "drying out". Ever since the accident and concussion, I'd get terrible headaches whenever I tried. I had two choices, quit or fight close to my natural weight.

I insisted to him that I had to move forward. He disagreed with me and said to me sternly, "If ya wanna be in the Golden Gloves, you'll be doing it without me. I can't be part of this." Just a few months before the Golden Gloves started, Al stepped away and I was given the choice to quit or go at it alone. My intuition told me to keep going, so I ignored Al's advice and filled out the application. All the beatings I took and all the training I did, couldn't be for nothing. The only solace I found, was from a handful of friends at work who still supported me. Everyone else thought it was a joke. I'd go to the gym and Al had his back turned to me again. My parents also continued to try and convince me not to go through with it. In the end, I was doubtful I'd even pass the physical for the competition. If that happened, at least I tried and was forced out medically instead of quitting.

When it came time for the physical, the doctor had an NYPD pin on his lapel. Not knowing the inner workings of the police department, I told him my dad was a retired cop and asked if he was. He laughed and replied, "No, I'm an honorary police surgeon," then resumed asking me about my medical history. I wound up passing the physical and my bloodwork came back perfect. The entire endeavor was a runaway train at this point, and there was nothing to stop me. I was being pulled in a direction by something, with or without support, and with or without the ability to win.

Chapter 9:
The Golden Gloves

In the last couple of months leading up to the fight scheduled during February of 2001, I tried to take Al Gavin's advice by dropping some weight. When I sent my application in to compete, I checked off the 168lb weight class. I made an honest effort to try and get back to my old fighting weight. It wound up being a terrible mistake on my part. By working too hard and trying to lose weight naturally, I overtrained and wound up getting some nagging injuries just before the fight.

The most serious one was to my right hand when I did something to the ligaments, requiring a soft cast for a few weeks. My injury-prone body, no thanks to the antibiotic that kept haunting me, was beginning to unravel with heavy training. Twinges in both shoulders, aches in my knees, and a permanent "stitch" in my ribs, forced me to shut it all down for a few weeks. I told my friends at work, the only ones who supported me, that I may not be able to fight. My weight crept up slowly without the intense training. 168lbs became an unreachable goal with only a couple of weeks to go. Regardless of it all, I still refused to quit.

Quitting wasn't an option for me, since it would prove my parents and other naysayers right. I returned to the gym and trained lightly so that my weight didn't continue to creep up. Just like if I had been disqualified medically, if I didn't make weight, there was no shame in it considering I was injured just before the fight. With about 30 people coming to see me, some having high hopes, I took the risk of them being sent home without watching me in the ring.

Fight day had arrived, and I was not feeling 100% physically. I felt weak, tired, and most of all, nervous. It was a long drive as I trekked out to Brooklyn with a million thoughts going through my head. Even though Al Gavin wasn't working with me anymore, I tried to keep some of his advice in my head, but everything popping up was negative. I was also nervous about showing up alone and without a trainer, which is a big "No-no" in a competition of this scale.

When I showed up at the church where the event was being held, I was sent downstairs to weigh-in and hang out for hours-on-end. Just like the drive from Long Island to Brooklyn, the hours may as well have been days. They were not happy I showed up without a cornerman. Just as in criminal court when you can't afford a lawyer, one was appointed for me. The trainer walked over, looked me up and down, and shook his head saying, "I sure hope you know what you're doing." Quite honestly, I didn't know. All I knew was that I had to do this no matter the cost.

When I stepped on the scale for the official weigh-in, I weighed in at 175lbs. For the first round of competition, they allowed 3lbs in either direction. Obviously, I was way out of range for the 168lb class, so they put me on standby as they jumbled things around for the 178lb'ers. I sat there and waited, hoping they'd find an opponent for me so my friends in the audience weren't sent home.

"Hey!" another fighter said, coming up to me and sitting down. "Looks like it's you and me," he cheerfully said. I breathed a sigh of relief as not only did I get an opponent, but he was even shorter than I was and seemed "soft" personality-wise. I was cordial to him, all while mapping out a strategy in my head to get through

THE GOLDEN GLOVES

this first fight. I thought to myself, "Alright, I'll keep him off with my jab all night, outpoint him, go home, and continue to recover, because I feel like garbage!" He sat there with a big goofy smile on his face, not knowing what I had planned for him.

They called his name over to the table, so he stood up and walked over there. When he was done, he came back, shook my hand, and said, "Sorry, they put me with somebody else." "Well, who's my new opponent?" I asked. He pointed across the floor to this towering mass who looked like an upside-down triangle. I don't know what my complexion looked like since I didn't have a mirror, but I felt like I had turned pale green. My game plan was out the window, and all I could think about was survival, not victory.

As the evening went on and I sat there for what felt like a million hours, the fighters began to make their way up 2 by 2 with the matches starting. On one side of the room, there was me. I was overtrained, overtired, hungry, thirsty, and nervous as hell. On the other side, my opponent was staring at me. He looked like a white version of Tommy Hearns, but more muscular with piercing blue eyes. It was obvious I was there at my natural "walk-around" weight, while he dried out to make 178lbs. It was a mismatch before it even started.

We got called and I began the long walk to the electric chair in front of my friends, family, and girlfriend. The crowd cheered as if they were in the Roman Coliseum about to watch a scrawny dissident get fed to a lion. "Let's put on a good show," I remember saying to him. He mumbled something back, but I couldn't hear what he said. We met up in the center of the ring, then went back to the corner. I shouldn't have, but I looked at my friends. All their faces, even the ones who supported me and knew I could fight, had a worried look on their face. "Just do the best you can," the rent-a-cornerman said to me. I looked at him with lasers in my eyes and said, "Thanks."

The bell rang and we both leapt out at each other. You could immediately see the size and reach advantage of my opponent. He held his arms far away from his body to keep me away. His arms were so long, it was as if he could reach all the way across the ring and contact anything he wanted. He was also overwhelmingly stronger, and able to dictate the pace of the fight with his looming presence.

Within the first few seconds of the fight, the action started. Forgive me if I can't remember all the details since he probably gave me a concussion, or I blocked it out of my memory. What I do remember is that within the first 10-20 seconds of the fight, he threw a punch that I deflected with my left glove, and I felt a ripping pain in my left shoulder.

I immediately switched to southpaw, leading with my right hand and snapping out a few jabs to keep him at bay. The sad part of it all, was knowing that if we had fought when I was 20 years old, it may have been a much easier night for me. I had more tricks up my sleeve, and all he had was his size and strength. However, I wasn't 20 years old anymore, and he whooped my ass. He kept crashing through my defense as I had no ability to truly defend myself with my left shoulder defunct.

With his hands held out so far away from his body, I decided to take advantage of the opening and his aggression. "I'm gonna draw him in and hit him up the middle with an uppercut," I said to myself during the fast-paced action. I began to back up towards the ropes to draw him in and he fell for the trap. Bam! I came through with my uppercut, snapping his head back. He just looked at me and dug a hook right into my kidney, lifting my feet up off the ground. At that moment, I knew I had no chance. I had just hit a home run off his head with my heavy hands, and he stared back at me. Al Gavin was right, if I couldn't knock my opponent out, I was going to lose.

In the chaos of me trying to stave him off and thinking of a way to survive, I also got a couple of "standing 8 counts'" as he nearly knocked me down. I didn't go down and there were a few fleeting moments where some of my friends had hope. After the second "8 count", I was tired of being embarrassed. I rushed aggressively at my opponent, cutting off the ring, and trapping him in the corner.

A few good shots landed on him and for a second, I had him on the ropes in a panic. He regrouped quickly by taking advantage of my smaller stature, steering me aside, and slipping away. Now it was me against the ropes and he charged in. Snap! I threw the hardest left jab I had in the arsenal in spite of my shoulder being injured. His head snapped back and I stunned him, but I was too rusty to notice it and let him off the hook. There was one more volley on his part and the ref stepped in to stop the action. I could hardly lift my left arm anymore to defend myself and that was it, it was over.

I walked back to my corner, shaking my head in defeat and being overwhelmed. The corner man said to me, kicking me while I was down, "Do you even know what you're doing? You wasted my time!" I looked at him with disdain and walked past him, climbing out of the ring. One of the first things said to me, and I can't remember if it was a friend or family member, was, "I told you not to do it." I felt like a loser and physically battered. The only relief I could find, was that I wasn't beaten as bad as the first sparring match during my comeback.

I walked back downstairs, and it was the loneliest walk one could take. My left shoulder felt like it had a hot knife through it, and my head was ringing from taking "Drago's" punches. Regardless, there was no blood, no scuff marks on my face, and I was still alive. "Good fight, man," my opponent said after coming up to me. "Sorry about what happened, you got me with some good shots," he said in a moment of good sportsmanship. "Thank you, good luck in the next round," I gracefully replied.

I got dressed, splashed my face with cold water, and went back upstairs to see my friends and family. They all gave me that "awww I'm sorry" look and patted me on the back; then my girlfriend offered to drive me home. The pride in me took over and I said, "No, I'm fine, let's just go home." I drove home, not saying a word. My hands were still shaking from the adrenaline and probably being concussed.

For the next few days, I just slept, slept, and slept some more. I went to the doctor to get my shoulder looked at. He said it seemed as if I had a partial tear of my rotator cuff. I made an appointment to get an MRI, but I didn't show up. I was so dejected, and it didn't matter anymore. It was over. I don't know what I was thinking, but for a moment, I thought I could win and recapture something stolen from me that night in my car accident.

Throughout this period, even my mom got in on the action and told me she knew I'd lose. It was a painful time as a young adult, and people took sport in kicking me while I recovered mentally and physically. Over the course of the next several weeks, my opponent went on to crush everyone they put in front of him. In retrospect, even with my body broken, overtrained, and injured, I put up a better fight against him than anyone else in the competition so far. He wound up making it to the finals, and my friends had a newfound respect for me.

My opponent's success helped me regain some confidence, and I returned to the boxing gym to keep myself in shape. Al Gavin became my friend after that, and we would casually talk about boxing as I hit the bag. Things were different now; my mindset had changed, and I was in a better place mentally. There was a sense of peace about me as the need to recapture something was gone. It was all about keeping in shape, healing, and moving forward. Al invited me to take part in some easy in-house bouts, and I won all 3 of them. It was because I was more relaxed and not worried about success or making weight. They wound up being the last boxing matches I ever had. Even in victory and not getting hit much, my shoulder was still a problem, and I started getting bad headaches.

The green light had taken me on a journey to defeat, healing, peace, and learning about myself. I also learned more about my friends, family, and girlfriend. However, it still felt like it took me to a dead end, and I didn't know why. With every answer, there were new questions.

Chapter 10: September 11, 2001

Monday September 10th was a normal day for all of us in the Northeast and throughout the Country. As for me, I spent most of my Mondays on the water with "Reel Nuts" before I was due in for work at 3pm. It was a good escape from the boat traffic since weekends were usually a madhouse along the south shore of Long Island. I did my usual run out to Debs Inlet off Far Rockaway that Monday. The fluke were leaving soon, so I tried to get some fishing in before they left for the season.

The Twin Towers were a familiar sight and that day was no different. I got so used to it and hardly paid them much attention anymore. The water was dead flat, and it was a very warm morning for September. There's an old saying that goes, "red skies at night, sailors delight; red skies in the morning, sailors take warning." Sometimes it rings true, but it's mostly by chance. Typically, a red sky in the morning is caused by cloud cover, and we had red skies that morning as the sun rose up through the clouds.

I fueled up the boat, picked up some bait, and started to make my way west down Reynolds Channel. The boat ran perfectly as I skimmed along the water as flat as glass. As the sun notched a little higher in the sky and broke through some of the clouds, it hit the Twin Towers and lit them up temporarily. It was the first time I had noticed them in a while, and it was the last time I ever saw them.

There's no reason to rehash the timeline and events of September 11th since there are countless books and videos on the subject. There's also no need to sanitize it either. What came for many was very ugly. We all had a "gut check" in the aftermath, and some went in different directions than others.

After the attack, the horizon glowed red at night as if the city had gotten hit with a nuclear weapon. The acrid smell of an electrical fire or burning electronics filled the air. I sat on the hood of my car, miles away, staring out at the destruction towards the west. I got back into my car and drove around aimlessly during the unseasonably warm September night. There was no official death toll or enemy to fight yet, just utter shock.

My drive took me to an American flag-lined street of an unknown town somewhere on the north shore of Long Island. To this day, I still can't remember where I was, where I went, or how I got home. My car sat at a red light with nobody on the streets. The neon sign of a pub adjacent to me, called my name. I parked the car on the empty street and walked in. Heads were hung low, TVs were off, and music played at a low volume from the jukebox. I ordered a burger and a beer, sat down at a booth by myself, and contemplated my next move.

A drunk man in a flannel shirt lifted his head up and yelled to the bartender, "Would you shut that damn music off?!" She quickly came around the bar, ran across the checkered floor, and unplugged the jukebox. The drunk man stood up and started to give an incoherent speech while crying. Someone started chanting, "USA! USA!" and we all joined in. At the moment, I didn't know what was going on, but out of the pile of molten steel and absolute sorrow, lives were being shaped and reshaped.

SEPTEMBER 11, 2001

I continued to drink until the 8th grader in me, the one unable to walk away from a fight, came out to fight once more. It was in that booth, at an unknown bar, where I concluded that my life was worthless and had no meaning. All these people were gone and loved ones were crying for them. Had it been me, would anybody miss me? Would anybody care? The honest answer to that question in my mind was no. My life up until that point was all about me and trying to pursue the next "thing" by checking off boxes. It was time to do something and help others. It was a "noble" moment, and it felt good inside knowing I was about to make some changes, but reality hit hard over the next few weeks.

Life went on as did school and work. I showed up to school every day as one should, and the acrid smell continued to fill the air. The showroom floor at work was empty, with no customers coming in unless they had a trivial problem. I'd watch them complain and all I could see was their lips moving without hearing what was coming out of their miserable mouths. Thousands of lives were gone, and here's this person nagging me that their $39 phone has static because they were too cheap to buy a real one.

I wanted to jump out of my own skin. "This is not what life is all about," I said to myself. Things got even worse as my bank account started to bleed profusely with no money coming in. Hardly any of my regular customers were coming by, and school bills were piling up. My customers weren't coming in because half of them were dead, and I wasn't aware of it yet. I only found out later, as previous orders and deliveries were rejected by grieving widows who had just lost everything. Everyone in the New York City Metro Area was impacted in one way or another, and we all knew someone who was killed. For me, it was in the hundreds, but one stood out to me more than the rest.

In the following weeks, I was given the news that my friend, Ezra, was killed. Ezra and I worked together for a year at Circuit

City when I had left P.C. Richard & Son for a short time. Ezra was one of the kindest people you'd ever meet. He started working at Circuit City when he was laid off from his job in NYC. Ezra got his job back a few months before 9/11, getting called to his death.

I distinctly remember all of us going to the city in a limousine for an award ceremony at the Marriott. It was for a job-well-done as he and I ranked high in sales for the company. He had a beautiful family, and his wife was pregnant at the time. I can't forget the image of him smiling with his kids and his beautiful wife, glowing with her baby bump, excited for their new edition to come. Finding out he was gone and his wife a widow, made me question my faith. In a moment of anger and sadness, I rejected the green light and all the other things that helped me along the way. It was about to come back to teach me a very big, very life-altering lesson.

Life at home with my girlfriend also took a big hit. Between the two of us and other outside forces, the behavior from all parties took a toll, and we broke up. She sent me packing and I never moved back into the house again. We had 2 cats together that we got as kittens, so I did my best to swing by and help. It kept us in touch constantly, which caused our breakup to become a relationship that was on and off for a couple of more years. It became the "zombie apocalypse" of relationships. The entire thing was dead. We just didn't know it and kept limping forward.

Work and school also suffered from my mindset after that fateful day. My sales numbers were low due to half of my clientele being gone, and nobody wanting to spend money. In school, all I did was worry about how I was going to pay my bills. Thankfully the Mazda was paid off and still alive. With 125,000 miles on it at this point and virtually worthless, I got the least amount of insurance on it to try and save money.

SEPTEMBER 11, 2001

On another front, I started getting severe nightmares on a level I wouldn't wish on anyone. It all started when I told one of my friends that I wasn't sure if I believed in God or angels anymore. He was shocked knowing some of the things I went through, but he was a skeptic himself. The conversation took a dark turn when we started poking fun at the idea of a supreme being. I'm guessing it wasn't a very good idea on my part, but the next set of events shook me to my core.

The word "night terror" would be a mild way to describe the level of dreams I was having since being kicked out of my girlfriend's, mocking God, and going through all the stresses many were going through after the attack. I'd close my eyes, and, in an instant, I was taken to the World Trade Center. Every night was a new floor, new location, and new body. Similar to me traveling outside of my body to my girlfriend's house and into her bedroom back in 1998, I was being transferred into actual victims of September 11th.

Executives, secretaries, fire fighters, EMTs, police, you name it; I experienced the entire horror from their perspective. I was burned alive, crushed, choked to death by smoke, choked to death by dust, and sometimes I'd even jump to my death. Most people wake up from their dreams before they die, but in every dream, I wound up dying. I felt their panic, pain, and souls leaving their bodies, before waking up in my bed. It was enough to drive someone mad, and I contemplated suicide. I wanted it to turn off and I yelled in my bed one night, "Leave me alone!"

There was one more dream to be had, and this was the most vivid one of all. I was an FDNY firefighter climbing up the stairs with a hose to bring water up to a floor. It was so hot, you could see the heatwaves rippling in the air. My protective gear was melting, and a hotter blast of air hit me when I opened the door at the top of the landing. The entire floor was mangled steel. Flames rode up the sides of the wall while being sucked into a hole through the ceiling.

I started putting water on it to no avail, but I kept trying. The ground started to shake below me, and everything gave way as I fell to my death. I was crushed by the collapsing tower and incinerated by the heat. Everything went black, then bright white with a voice saying, "Fight for us, Ben." I woke up screaming and my clothes soaked through with sweat. My skin was still burning and my bones still hurting from being crushed; that's how real it was.

When I heard the words, "Fight for us, Ben," I thought it was telling me to enlist in the service. With my girlfriend and I having the problems we did, and everything else going to shit, I went to speak to a recruiter. He told me it was unlikely they'd take me due to my old injuries; plus the shape my joints were in from the post-surgical infection 3 years prior. As I walked out of the office, he said to me as the door was closing, "If you wanna help, go be a cop or something." It was out of character for a recruiter to try and convince someone to do something else. I took it as a message and began to listen again to the mysterious forces guiding me towards wherever I was going.

The awful dreams finally stopped, but I had a long way to go convincing others to see things as I did.

Chapter 11: Talk the Talk

About 6 or 7 months after September 11th, and immediately after my encounter with the military recruiter, I decided to have a talk with my dad. It wasn't about the strange dreams or feeling that I was being pulled in a direction. Neither he nor my mom believed in that stuff. It was a direct and to-the-point talk, because I feared I'd be met with fierce resistance. From the day he told me he'd "break my legs" back in 1982, till just a year prior to the attack, he had pounded it into my head to stay away from "the job".

I decided to wait until we were out on the boat, so that he couldn't brush me off and walk away. Without anywhere to go except for a swim back to shore, he'd be "trapped" and forced to finish the conversation. I was also best on the water thinking-wise and quicker on my feet with my mind more at ease. Only a month prior, I had gotten the boat ready for the new season. The day I picked to ask my dad out, was a typical and horrible Long Island early spring day.

My dad was in a bad mood already due to the weather. I was nervous to have the talk, but there was no choice. We decided to take a ride and burn some fuel to get all the winterizing agent out of the engine. We took "Reel Nuts" westward down a familiar route across Reynolds Channel. He insisted on being the captain that day, taking the boat into the chop and stiff breeze on purpose for dragging him out.

My teeth chattered as I hid behind the windshield as best as I could to stay warm. The loud engine and howling wind made it hard for us to have a talk, so I waited until we got to the 5mph zone by the Long Beach Bridge. "Dad, I wanna be a cop," I blurted out. He looked at me and stopped the boat. "I'm tired of doing this. I need to do something. I need to help," replying to myself because he didn't say a word. "I'm taking the next test," I continued, as his head turned forward to look ahead.

He brought the throttle back up, not saying a word, and continued towards Debs Inlet. "I'm 26 years old. I'm a grown man and I'm doing this," I said loudly through the wind, buzzing engine, and chop slapping up against the aging hull. There was still no reply as he forged forward and stood motionless like a marble statue. We got to the Atlantic Beach Bridge, and he slowed down for the next 5mph zone; then we went to the edge of the inlet.

My dad gazed out at where the Twin Towers used to be, gripping the steering wheel hard until his knuckles cracked. He turned his head, looked at me, and said, "Ok, Ben, but you have to listen to my advice in order to get through everything." My dad had a stone-cold serious face on him as he spoke. He whipped the boat around and headed east. With the wind and chop to our backs, we took a smooth ride home. "When is the test?" he asked. I told him that it was some time in the fall, and I wasn't sure of the exact date yet. All I knew was that there was a June test and I had missed the deadline. However, the wait for the new test wasn't very long since they needed more cops.

It went much better than I thought, and it was obvious the events during September changed things. My dad had finally set me free. In my mind, I had "permission" to pursue what I was always meant to do. The next few weeks with my dad consisted of long talks about the NYPD, what to expect, and him reminiscing about his time as a cop. We talked about the academy, patrol, the dangers involved, and how to navigate the toxic internal issues of the NYPD.

Convincing my on-and-off girlfriend was another thing. In the end, it didn't really matter since I was going through with it anyway. However, I wanted to gauge her reaction to see if we had a future. Initially, she was supportive because she didn't know how much life would change for me after taking the oath. Even with her support, though, I could still feel a level of hesitation on her part. Most of it stemmed from her childhood memories of cops knocking on the door whenever her parents got into a fight.

After making the rounds and talking to my dad, girlfriend, and friends, life began to stabilize as if I had satisfied the Universe. I remained in school, sales at the store picked up, money started flowing back in, and I was on steady ground again. In fact, sales picked up to the point where I made more money than I ever did. It was as if the forces in play were insulating me; preparing me for the big pay cut I was about to take if I got into the academy.

During October of 2002, test time had arrived. I don't remember the exact date of it, but I remember the circumstances and details very clearly. That's because I was suffering from a bad case of the flu, and New York City was being pounded by a wicked nor'easter. I was in such bad shape, and my dad had to drive me into the city like a child being dropped off at school. I laid down in the back seat, curled up in the fetal position, and shivered as the 103 degree fever dominated my body.

We pulled up next to the school near One Police Plaza and I opened the door. The wind flung it open as tiny drops of heavy rain blew inside the car. My bones creaked as I got up and exited to get in the line. The next half hour was spent standing in the rain and wind, begging God to take me because I was so miserable. When they finally let us in, I squeaked down the hallway with my wet sneakers and into a classroom. My clothes sounded like an oversaturated sponge when my butt hit the seat of the desk.

I was in such bad shape, I said, "fuck it," to myself and breezed through the test as fast as I could without double-checking my work. I just wanted to go home and die. My dad met me at the curb, and I climbed back into the car, resuming the fetal position in the back seat. "How did you do?" he asked. I just groaned and went to sleep. It was a long ride home due to traffic on the Belt Parkway, shaken awake by every puddle-filled pothole we crashed into.

When we got home, I dragged myself inside, popped some meds, and slept some more. As I drifted off to sleep during that cold, rainy, and windy October night, I had another very odd dream. I was sitting in a crowded classroom in the academy, in uniform, and waiting for the instructor to come in. A girl sitting in front of me with brown hair, slightly turned my way without revealing her face, and handed me a pencil. When I thanked her, she laughed and replied, "Of course, you're my husband."

I woke up with my clothes soaking wet due to the fever breaking. "That was odd," I thought to myself. Not knowing anything about the academy and my dad cautioning me about females on the job, I blew it off as a fever dream and didn't think much about it. A couple of months later, I got a post card in the mail with my test score. I was ranked high on the list even though I took the test half-dead. Things were happening very fast, and they were about to happen even faster.

Chapter 12: Walk the Walk

In the upcoming months, I was called for my background check, physical examination, and fitness test. The overall process was a lot tougher back then. The city was overflowing with candidates looking to take the oath after September 11th. It afforded them the ability to pick and choose who they wanted. The only difference was that compared to previous years, they were in "express mode". The NYPD had to fill the ranks quickly, since cops were retiring at a high rate since the attack.

It was a major pain in the ass as they wanted every single detail about my life. They wanted so much information that the packet was about 2 inches thick. It felt as if they wanted me to tell them what I was doing when I was swimming around in my dad's testicles. Every job, every ticket, every accident, and every address I ever lived at, had to be provided. Reaching back that far was a hassle, but my dad kept me going by reminding me that everything with the NYPD is a test. Anything perceived as "negative" required an essay explaining what happened, why, and the result.

"Hurry up and wait" was a term my dad used a lot throughout the process. It's something that I quickly became used to as they demanded information on-the-spot from you, or had you show up somewhere at a certain time. After giving you short notice to be at a location, they'd make you wait for hours in a line. It was all part of the test to see how much information you can provide, or how much they can inconvenience you, before you break and quit. This is how they weeded out the candidates before you got to the next step.

Each step was even harder and more intrusive. The department psychologist hounded me about the relationship with my girlfriend, and not living together anymore. I understand that they were trying to uncover any domestic violence or other problems, but even things that weren't a big deal, they made into one to see how I'd react.

"I see here you went back to your parents after living with your girlfriend," the psychologist said. "Yes, we broke up and I'm there until I see if I'm getting into the academy or not," I replied. She snapped back, "Well, this might be a problem, you moving out and all." I looked at her dumbfounded and asked, "Did you marry your first boyfriend?" "Ummm, no?" she replied with a surprised look as I turned the questions on her. "Well, there you go," I said and added, "Neither did I." After the exchange, she hurried me out of the office. I found out later that I passed the psychological part of The Inquisition.

The next step, the obstacle course, was extra special. While it should've been easy for me and was for most, the course made me question life as I knew it. On a frigid February morning in 2003, I sat in an RMP outdoors with the windows down and the engine off. I was waiting to get called to run into the gym to do the course. You started in the patrol car, ran inside, jumped a fence, and ran the course. After completing the course, you had to run up the stairs and drag a weighted dummy across the hallway to the finish line.

I sat there and waited, then waited some more. With the engine off, there was no heat and the temperature outside was in the low teens. For the test, I was wearing just shorts and a t-shirt. There was a problem ahead of me, with someone failing the test. I honestly think they forgot all about me, and I was probably in the car for about 30 minutes. With my teeth chattering and my body frozen stiff, the gym door opened, and the instructor yelled, "Go!" I barely got the door open to the car and ran into the gym, pulling every muscle in my legs.

When my foot hit the bowed-out fence, worn out from everyone else climbing it, it slipped, and my leg pounded onto the floor. It felt as if lightning hit my leg and I had no power to get myself over the fence. Determined not to fail, I pulled myself over with my arms. In the process, I pulled every muscle in my arms and shoulders. I refused to quit, completing the course, and getting to the stairs. My legs were dead due to the sudden start in the cold, and my arms were dead from pulling my 180lb body over the fence.

As I got to the stairs, feeling like a rhinoceros tranquilized by several darts to the legs and arms, I tried to figure out how to get up. The instructor was at the top of the landing, laughing at me, waving his hands toward him while saying, "C'mon, c'mon, you can do it," in a condescending way. I grimaced at him, pulled myself up the stairs, and dragged the dummy across the finish line. I wasn't close to the time limit, but it sure felt like it.

For the next 2 weeks, I could hardly walk or lift my arms. Suddenly moving after being encased in ice, resulted in pulling almost every muscle in my body. Everything hurt, from my toes to my balls. Even my ears were aching. I passed the test, but at a cost, and I was wondering what I was doing or if it was worth it. However, the next test was the biggest one of all.

During the entire process and close to the timing of the obstacle course, I waited in another long line out in the cold. This one was outside of Lefrak City in Queens, where we had the medical exam. In the line with me was a 20-year Marine and Gulf

War Veteran. He was very excited to be there and had a lot to say. I knew almost everything about him, even his blood type, as we stood there, victims of "hurry up and wait". When we got inside, they handed us another 2-inch-thick packet to fill out, and "Gunny" continued to chew the fat. "You're with me, now," he said. "I'll get you prepared for this," saying as if he was sure we'd be in the same class.

He was wrong, I wasn't with him. On that cold winter day, my NYPD aspirations came to a screeching halt and dashed within an instant. After giving them my medical history, I was immediately put on the "medical review" pile of candidates. This is where candidates went to "die" back then since they had plenty of healthier recruits to pick from.

I couldn't believe it. I thought I was following my path after having those horrible dreams and taking advice from the military recruiter. Everything I had done up until this point felt like it was for nothing. I began to go over options in my head since I was still in school, able to fall back on my current job, and still working towards a degree. I came home upset and told my dad what happened. He said to me, "How can you pass the physical for the Golden Gloves and not for this?"

I started to think about what he said, and then I remembered the doctor who did my Golden Gloves physical. He had that NYPD lapel pin on him, and he said he was an honorary police surgeon. I dug through my old boxing paperwork, looking for any information on the doctor, and I couldn't find anything. I found a few other contact numbers and started making some calls the next day. Finally, I came across someone who had the doctor's info, and I called him. I told him what was going on and he said, "Don't worry about it, I'm going to write a letter to the board and we're going to get this fixed." I gave him the contact information, and he wrote the letter. He explained to them that if I could train, pass the physical, and fight in the Golden Gloves, I could easily get through the academy.

A few weeks later, I was taken off of medical review and allowed to proceed to the next step. At this point, I couldn't deny what was going on in my life. The entire purpose of being in the Golden Gloves was for this moment. I had to fight, I had to lose, and I had to ignore all the naysayers. Just as with the NYPD and their petty tests, I was being tested in real life to see if I was worthy for this journey.

Chapter 13:
The Actual Hangover

During the entire process of potentially being hired by the NYPD, life remained somewhat normal. School, work, and life with my friends continued onward. Every year my buddies and I would pick an epic vacation during school break. It was easy since work never denied me time off during the summer due to being a student. This year was no different, and for late June of 2003, we picked Las Vegas as our destination.

The last time I was in Vegas was back when we used it as a stopping-off point to go to my cousin's wedding in California. To this day, I'm still banned from the greater San Francisco area for getting drunk and taking one of the bridesmaids back to my room. It caused a big scene, but the big lesson here was how to play blackjack. My dad taught me so well, I used blackjack to help pay for school and books down in Atlantic City every other weekend. Just like with alpacas and other farm animals, that's all for another book.

The trip to Vegas was set, and rumors started flying around about getting called for the January 2004 police academy. I began discussing it with my supervisors at work that May. They were shocked I was looking to leave after the year I was having income-wise. If I got called for the academy, I was choosing to take a major pay cut on a scale which looked foolish. By taking the oath,

I would've accepted an annual salary half of what I made during the first 5-6 months of 2003 alone.

They were about to lose one of their top salesmen and offered me everything but the kitchen sink to stay. I turned down every offer that got more ridiculous as time went on. While I enjoyed working there and had a great boss, I wasn't going to be tempted away from the forces guiding me towards something else. I was done fighting the Universe and getting my ass kicked, so it was full steam ahead.

June arrived quickly and my friend and I boarded the plane for Vegas. Since we were college students, everything had a strict budget. The only thing we did "big" was rent a Lincoln Town Car to cruise the boulevard in style. Everything else was tame. We had a cheap room, no reservations at restaurants, and a small amount of money put aside for playing blackjack. Things were about to take a drastic turn when we landed in the airport.

I'd be lying if I said the first thing I did was turn my phone on when we got off the plane, because that's not what happened. I was so entranced by the slot machines in the airport by the gate, that I walked over like a victim of the Pied Piper's music, and fed it 5 dollars. The wheels of the slot machine spun, landing on nothing, and there went my 5 bucks. I shrugged and walked away with a goofy sucker's smile back to my friend, Sean.

I reached into my pocket, turned my phone on, and it said I had 7 voicemails. This was back in the day before smartphones and any true texting ability. I had no idea what was going on. The voicemails were from my girlfriend, parents, and the NYPD. They were all trying to get in touch with me. First, I called my parents, and they told me the NYPD was looking for me. My girlfriend said the same, so I gave them a call.

It was my background investigator looking to see if I was still interested in being an NYPD cop. I told her yes, then she explained to me that I was on the "backfill" list for the July 2003 academy. They were just waiting on the mayor to make a final decision on the size of the class. She told me to be prepared to be sworn in on Tuesday July 1st. The trip to Vegas we had planned nearly 6 months ago, was June 26th into the weekend. It wound up being my last weekend as a civilian.

After going into a corner and away from the noise of the slot machines to make my phone calls, I rushed back to Sean and told him the news. We shook hands and gave hugs as he congratulated me. "What do we do now?" Sean asked. I replied with a devilish voice and smile, "Go out in style." He looked at me in fear as to what was to come, but in the end, I wasn't the only ingredient that got this "dumpster fire" lit.

The only thing I didn't change was the car. Our Lincoln was a perfect ride for the next 4 days. When we got to the hotel, I upgraded the room we were sharing. Sean said, "Ben, I can't afford this, man." I replied, "Relax, I'm picking up the difference." Everything went off the rails and you can feel my bank account shrinking with every bad decision. The way I looked at it, it was like my trip to Florida as a kid when I was about to get the invasive surgery on my hands. I was nervous about what was to come, and life was going to change in a big way. It was a trip into the unknown, so I may as well live it up and enjoy life.

A few other friends met us down in Vegas and avoided me in fear; mostly due to some wild stories about me from the past. However, Sean stuck around to "babysit" me. The phone rang in the room as we were unpacking. It was our other friends telling us they were going to a club and asked if we wanted to come along. Knowing I hated clubs, they got the answer they were looking for. "Nah, I'm good," I said and hung up the phone. "What are we doing?" Sean asked. I replied, "Let's play some blackjack."

I was always taught to read the room and the tables before sitting down. "Walk around and feel the energy," my dad once said. We took a few laps around the casino, then came across a rowdy bunch of guys cheering and yelling. The "shoe" (deck of cards) was hot, so we stuck around. You never enter mid-shoe if a table is hot, it's common courtesy. One of the guys saw me standing there, waiting for the correct time to sit down. He said to me, "C'mon! Play with us, kid!" The rest of them cheered on the invite, convincing me to sit.

They were big, burly guys, with tattoos all over their arms. They were as loud as the stereotypical New York City stockbroker, but they were of another breed. These were battle-hardened military guys and clearly, they were there to have some fun. I started winning some hands and making good decisions to keep the hot deck going. Every time the dealer would break, or the entire table won, they would reach across and give me an alcohol-soaked bear hug. These guys were twice my size, and I was losing oxygen with each hug.

I looked at the guy next to me and said, "Thank you for your service." He looked at me and said, "Thanks, little guy, what do you do?" I told him about September 11th, losing friends, and how I got the news today that I was probably starting the NYPD academy Tuesday. The action stopped, they all looked at me, and the table went silent. "Waitress!" one of them yelled, "Get the entire table a round of Louis XIII, we have a new warrior with us." They all came around and shook hands, giving me more hugs and congratulatory pats on my head; all-while making sounds like a bunch of pirates.

"Arrrrgggh! You're with us now!" they exclaimed while jostling me around like a little kid. The drinks came and we all took shots of $200 per glass cognac. You don't do shots of cognac like this, but we did that afternoon. All Sean could do was watch what was unfolding. The dumpster fire was lit as they told me they were Navy SEALs. They had just gotten back from the theater and awaiting to get redeployed soon.

These guys had hard lives. They didn't know what the next day would bring, and I was along for the ride now. What was supposed to be a budget trip, turned into a circus with upgraded rooms, high-roller blackjack, expensive cognac, and a bunch of Navy SEALs who could drink 10 of me under the table. We broke away with our winnings for a bit, gave them my number, and proceeded to spend almost $1,000 for a steak dinner, cocktails, wine, and champagne. "What are you doing?" Sean asked. "Going out in style," I replied in my best semi-slurred Sinatra voice.

The Lincoln sat collecting dust in the garage. We had no choice but to take a cab wherever we went that night. The SEALs called us and had us meet at one of the local strip clubs. They were throwing money around and ordering expensive drinks. I decided to do the same as to not look like a big wuss in their eyes. Sean cautioned me one more time, but when I bought him a lap dance from one of the cutest little things in there, he was now along for the ride. The devil on his shoulder (me) won out.

The party continued every night. It was to the point where I turned to Sean and said, "If we don't stop, we're going to die." He looked at me, agreed, and we left the room as we ignored the phone ringing. Our last night was just the two of us. No girls, no other friends, no SEALs; just some nice whiskey, cigars, and more expensive food. There's an iconic picture of us that's still on my computer. We had bloodshot eyes from all the alcohol, half-lit cigars, glasses of whiskey, and what-looked-like cocaine strewn across the table. However, it was just the light of the flash picking up the dust and pitting of the glass surface.

It was an awesome trip and my last one as a civilian. Overall, I spent almost everything I had in my bank account, plus all my winnings. What was supposed to be a budget trip, turned into a 4-day bender spent on the best alcohol, best cigars, best food, best strip clubs, and best hotel room they had available. I came home with my net worth consisting of $700 and the same beat-up Mazda with 140,000 miles on it. There was just enough money to be sworn in that Tuesday, and for the required uniforms the following week. I also received a consolation prize, a hangover that lasted for 7 additional days.

As for the Navy SEALs, I still wonder to this day where they are and who survived, if any.

PART III

Chapter 14: The Wool Suit

"**Ten-hut!**" a police academy instructor yelled across the basketball courts of Queens College. After I got home from Vegas the day before, I received the final call at night confirming I was to be sworn in. Over 1,600 of us lined up on the blacktop during a hot summer Tuesday morning. The instructor called "attention" to be inspected. A female officer with a long "rack" of medals, crisp uniform, and hair pulled back in a ponytail, paced back and forth to single-out anyone she deemed "worthy". Her hair was pulled back so tight, her eyebrows were 2 inches higher than they should be.

"Recruit!" she yelled at one victim. "Why aren't you in business attire?!" she barked again. The poor kid in jeans, button-up shirt, and tie, shrugged with indifference. "Go home!" the academy instructor yelled loud enough so that everyone could hear it. One by one, she sent recruits home, never to be heard from again. They were eliminated right then and there for seemingly being unprepared. Another recruit decided to take advantage of being an EMT previously, using his parking plaque to park closer than anyone else could.

"Whose car is this?!" the female instructor screamed like a banshee. Nobody came forward to claim their car. "If this is nobody's car, I guess we can tow it since it's in an unauthorized spot!" she exclaimed. In almost an instant, a recruit broke ranks and hurriedly walked across the blacktop of the basketball courts towards the instructor. "Congratulations! You're an EMT again! Go Home!" she screamed.

As I watched the bloodbath in my black wool suit on a hot summer morning, sweat dripped from every pore in my body. I closed my eyes, whispering to myself in prayer, "Please don't come near me, please don't come near me." If she had walked by and the sun caught me at the right angle, she'd be able to see the alcohol vapors from Vegas, rising out of my collar and any exposed skin. It was so bad, that if somebody walked by with a lit match or cigarette, I would've burst into flames as the instructors laughed while watching me broil. I feel bad for anyone who had to stand next to me as I reeked of scotch, tequila, rum, red wine, champagne, cigars, stripper's perfume, and bad decisions.

As the hot sun cooked us for another hour on the blacktop, I began to get the shakes and felt nauseous as the 2nd day of my hangover kicked in. "Don't faint, Ben. Don't faint," I said to myself, trying to keep it together. The female instructor kept walking up and down the line, sending recruits home one by one; still yelling loud enough to make the ground vibrate. When they felt they had done enough, we were called into the building.

1,600 of us walked up the stairs in a single file and through the doors of the auditorium. At the end of each aisle, was another recruit holding a sign with the assigned company number we were given. As I walked down the top of the stairs, deep into the belly of the auditorium, a familiar face was standing there with a card which read "Company 31". With a big grin on his face, shaking his head as if to say "yes", Gunny stood there like the cinderblock he was.

As I entered the aisle, he put his roast beef-clawed hands on my shoulder and said, "See? I told you so!" Even though he was

THE WOOL SUIT

scary, I felt a sense of relief since at least I knew someone. I found out later that he lived in East Meadow too, and we would wind up carpooling/taking the train into the city together. He was also the motivational force I needed to help get me through the academy and was picked to be our company sergeant. For the next couple of days, Queens College was our home as we sat through orientation, filled out paperwork regarding benefits, beneficiaries, and went over the countless expectations.

Gunny sat next to me, leaning over and saying, "Dude, what's wrong with you?" as he sniffed me. I replied with a simple answer, "Vegas." He chuckled as if that's all he needed explanation-wise. The 20 year Marine Veteran sat next to me every day and said my smell improved as time went on. We continued to go over paperwork as I met more of the fellow recruits in my company over the next few days. The instructors also informed us that we'd be off July 4th for the holiday. They proceeded to show us how to fill out a "28" (leave of absence form) because nothing is free, and they were about to take our 1st vacation day from us.

When we all got that initial call to show up at Queens College, it was driven home by the NYPD not to quit our jobs until we took the oath. My job knew what was going on, but now it was time to make the rounds, quit my old job at P.C. Richard & Son, and tell all my curious friends and family how it was going. Still suffering from a hangover and the wool suit sticking to my skin from the heat and humidity, I told the story repeatedly to anyone who asked. By the time everyone was satisfied, I wanted to burn the suit. However, there were a few more days to go as we didn't have uniforms yet.

On the last day at Queens College, the instructors told us where our next destination would be. We were to be at Floyd Bennett Field the following Monday to run 1.5 miles. They wanted to see where we were at standards-wise. "Enjoy your holiday weekend, recruits, because we own you now," an instructor said with a sadistic smile before dismissing us for the July 4th weekend.

Chapter 15: Vapor Lock

July 4th weekend after getting sworn into the NYPD, consisted of spending time with friends, family, and my on-and-off girlfriend. They were all congratulating me, and it was a nice weekend overall. The two things looming on my mind, remained my trek into the unknown, and the run we were about to partake in at Floyd Bennett Field. Previously, we had to do the 1.5 mile run to get accepted into the academy. However, this was a different animal overall, and not in a controlled environment.

I did the smart thing and stayed away from any alcohol. With every drink offered, I gagged and turned them down with the thoughts of my ongoing hangover. It didn't matter, though, the debauchery in Vegas would still haunt me for a few more days. The stage was set, and I was about to become a leper in the eyes of Gunny, the instructors, and my classmates.

Monday arrived and it was 95+ degrees on the old and abandoned tarmac of Floyd Bennett Field. We had 15 minutes to complete the 1.5 mile run, which was the same time to get accepted into the academy. However, with my age group, you had to complete it in 11 minutes and 15 seconds or so to graduate. With all the roadwork from boxing, I should've been ok. However, this was not the case thanks to me trying to keep up with those Navy SEALs a week prior.

They ran one recruit company at a time on the runway, while the remaining groups sat there like overcooked eggs in a frying pan. We were company 31, so 30 other companies ran before us as we sat there for hours. I'm sure some of us probably suffered from heatstroke, but I was probably the only one suffering from a secret bout of alcohol poisoning. Gunny turned to me and asked, "Are you alright?" "No," I replied with a dry mouth and shaking hands. "Don't worry," he said, "Just stay with me."

It was time to run, and I did my best to keep up with Gunny. His pace was like a bionic racehorse, unbothered by the heat. The runway was so long, I looked down towards the end and couldn't even see the instructor as the heatwaves distorted the view. If they were looking at me, the vapors of leftover alcohol probably made me look invisible too. Nonetheless, I pushed forward and kept up for the first mile with Gunny.

As I continued to run like an engine at high RPMs without any oil, my entire body seized up and stopped. Every single muscle went into spasm, and it felt as if I were stuck in cement. Gunny didn't even look back and kept running as if to say "Bye!" Other classmates started passing me, and all I could do was walk slowly. I wasn't out of breath or out of shape, I was in "vapor lock" from all the alcohol in Vegas.

An instructor ran towards me and got right in my face. "Why aren't you running? What's wrong with you?!" they screamed while trying to motivate me. There was nothing left I could do, and there was no amount of yelling that would get my muscles to unfreeze. If you started shooting at me or unleashed a hive of Africanized bees, I would've just accepted my fate, dying out there on the blistering hot tarmac. I crossed the finish line with a tortoise-like time of 17 minutes after running the first mile in under 7 minutes.

VAPOR LOCK

It was embarrassing and I didn't know what came next. I thought I was out of the academy, and the dream was over. Regret set in as I knew I took things too far on vacation. The instructors rounded up all the "slugs", including me, and told us that this was just a test. I was lumped in with all the recruits who were *actually* out of shape. We were all given a speech about losing weight, nutrition, and exercise. Gunny was disappointed in me, but I assured him it was just a one-off occurrence.

Due to my poor run, "remedial running" was waiting for me when we officially started the academy. It was comical and sad at the same time, but it was my fault. Thankfully that Monday was the last day of the hangover. Between the running and possible heatstroke, all the alcohol burned off and I was ready to start the next phase. Gunny was waiting for me at the train tracks the next morning, and the Universe was about to throw me another curveball.

Chapter 16: The Police Academy

Trains flew by the station in Bellmore, NY as we awaited the correct one to get to Penn Station. I was back in my hated wool suit and back in the heat, so the temporary whoosh of air from the speeding trains felt good. I stood there with Gunny, ready for the next step with a bunch of guys going to the same destination. We didn't know what to talk about as most of us had no idea what to expect. It was all mostly small talk, and we shared stories about what we did prior to the academy.

We came from all walks of life, and it was nice to hear that I wasn't the only one there because of September 11th. As we stood around bullshitting, a petite woman with brown hair in a gray suit walked up to us. Her arms were crossed as she shuffled over, holding a binder, and looking down at her feet with shyness and hesitation. "Are you guys going to the academy?" she asked while lifting her head up slightly. At the same time, we all grunted "Yes," then turned back around to talk to each other again. "Can I follow you guys in?" she replied. We turned back around, and all said at the same time while overlapping each other, "Yeah, yeah, sure, yeah," enthusiastically since she was cute.

I introduced myself and she told me her name was Jenn, while shyly looking down at her feet again and blushing. She began to warm up, and by the end of the train ride, she was joking with us as if she were one of the guys. It turned out that we were all from East Meadow, and I knew one of the recruit's older brothers from Woodland Junior High School. It was a perfect fit. I had a crew and were all inseparable from that moment on.

Our first week of the police academy in the main building, consisted of getting piles and piles of ditto sheets, plus the NYPD patrol guide. For those who have no idea about the guide, it's about as big as the Old and New Testament combined; filled with rules, regulations, and catch-all's to get you jammed up if they needed something to look for. We also took a subway ride into Brooklyn to order our academy uniforms and dress uniforms for when/if we graduated. Going forward, the wool suit was gone, and I was in uniform for the next 19 years.

After getting home from my first day in uniform, I decided to swing by the military recruiter in town and thank him for his advice. When I pulled into the lot, the storefront was empty with no signs of anything ever being there. I got out and walked up to the building with a look of confusion on my face as I turned around, looking everywhere. I stared up at the facade and there was nothing there, not even holes in the bricks where a sign would've been previously.

"Can I help you?" an older gentleman asked me as he exited his business to see what I was looking at. "Yeah, I was just wondering where the recruiting office went," I replied. "I'm sorry son, there hasn't been anything here for years," as he walked away and went back into his store. He stuck his head out and yelled, "Good luck in the academy, though!" and the door shut. I stood there confused for another few minutes. "I know I'm in the right spot," I said to myself. I got back in my car and proceeded to drive up and down the road in a panic until I gave up.

I returned home, took a shower, and collapsed in exhaustion with anticipation of the next day. Before waking up, I had a dream

THE POLICE ACADEMY

about the recruiter and his office. Usually, I could wake myself up out of a dream if I thought it was too weird. However, just like the 9/11 dreams, it wouldn't let me get out. I walked into the recruiting office, and the same recruiter was there. "Good! You listened! Now listen to the other dreams," he said with a smile on his face. My alarm went off and I woke up to catch the early morning train.

That morning, I was quiet as everyone else was chatting it up. All I could do was think about the dream, what it meant, and what happened to the recruiting office. "Was it just a dream? Where did I go to? I know it was real. I was making phone calls while riding around," I thought to myself as I tried to figure everything out. "Are you ok?" Jenn asked over the noise of the train traveling towards Penn Station. "Yeah, I'm fine, just tired," I said. "I'm not a morning person either," she replied. I just nodded my head and went back to being quiet.

The weird dreams and circumstances had to be set aside as the academy was getting real. I had to focus on my priorities. There was no way I was going to fail and go crawling back to my old job. I had to keep pushing forward. I also became a ghost to most of my friends and girlfriend since the academy took up all my time. I was either running, studying, at the academy, or sleeping. We were warned by instructors that civilians wouldn't understand, and they were right. Things were strained with my girlfriend, so I agreed to take her out east during a weekend to go apple picking, and to the shopping outlets.

Back in the academy, remedial running was short-lived since I didn't belong there in the first place. I was running laps around everyone else in the program. An instructor came up to me and yelled in my face, "Why are you here?!" "I don't know, sir!" I yelled back. I couldn't tell him that a 4 day bender locked up my muscles, because they would've lost their shit. "Go back to your company and get out of my face!" he yelled. "Yes sir!" I said in my best "academy voice". I rejoined the group, never returning to remedial running again.

Everything was going smooth, and it was time for the first test. Our group of locals from the academy decided to study together, but I couldn't go because of the promise I made to my girlfriend. As my crew studied and got ready for the test without me, my girlfriend and I took a ride to the North Fork of Long Island. The first stop was at the shopping outlets, where I happened to run into my academy sergeant.

My sergeant was out sick due to a broken arm. We had a brief and cordial conversation as my girlfriend stood there. I asked about her arm and if she's coming back soon. She explained to me how the department works when it comes to injuries, and my girlfriend started to fume. "That's your academy instructor?" my girlfriend asked as we walked away. "Yeah, why?" I replied. It was obvious she was upset because my academy sergeant was good looking, but I had zero control over that. She was mad at me for no reason, and the rest of the day got even more awkward.

As we were picking apples, a World War II era bomber flew over the field, then another, and another. It turned out that there was an airshow going on and the pilots were using the farm as their marker to turn back around. We had a personal and up-close view of some of the most beautiful, vintage aircraft. I stood there in awe as my apple basket was half-full. "Are you going to pick apples or what?" my girlfriend asked. She was still mad at me about my academy sergeant. As we drove from the North Fork back to her place, we didn't say a word.

In my mind, I knew that this was a bad sign of things to come, and that she couldn't handle me being in the academy. We had a lot of flaws in our relationship at this point, and the academy continued to expose what we already knew. I tried to ignore that day going forward, but I couldn't get it out of my head. All I could see is myself in the future, divorced with 2 kids, paying child support, and eating ramen noodles in somebody's basement apartment.

It wasn't easy dealing with the relationship drama all while trying to focus on the academy. This had been going on for far too long and over the course of several years now. Instead of allowing it to consume me, I retreated more into myself, focusing on the task at hand. Our first test had arrived. I was nervous since studying alone, but I wound up getting over a 90 on the exam. I was given a pass into the next stage of the academy, then disaster struck physically.

While it was nice that the doctor from the Golden Gloves helped get me into the academy, my body was still prone to injury due to my accident long ago; plus, what the antibiotics did to my muscles and ligaments. During the academy, they had us running on the wood floors at the gym in large groups. Lap after lap, sweat dripped onto the floors from 120+ individuals running in a very small space. The floor was very slippery, and somebody wiped out in front of us. A domino effect ensued, and about 20 of us went down, me included. My right leg went over my head, hyperextending my hip, and leaving me with a twinge every time I tried to run. It was bad enough where I had to go to the hospital, and they believe I did something to my hip flexor.

Running over the next couple of weeks became a challenge. Every time we'd run for more than a certain period, my right leg would go dead and all I could do was walk. There was no choice but to drop out of the run, all while getting yelled at and embarrassed by the instructors. I wasn't sure if I would make it, and my classmates were pressuring me as to why I kept dropping out. It wasn't about being out of shape, out of breath, or laziness. My leg would simply stop working at a moment of its choosing.

I tried to find every possible way to put less strain on the leg. This meant driving into the city more, instead of taking the train all the time. It afforded me less walking on the bad leg while hauling the heavy academy bag around Penn Station, to the subway, and then more blocks to the academy. Gunny, Jenn, and a few other people would carpool with me sometimes. Jenn wasn't in our company, but she was in the same squad and same days off, so we'd break off and go our separate ways when we got to the building.

She and I got to talking one day, and she said she was struggling in the gym as well. We were in separate gym blocks, so I didn't know what she was going through. Although Jenn was a sprinter in high school, she was having issues with asthma and controlling her breathing. This forced her to drop out of some of the runs, facing the same issues I did. We decided to help each other out, so that we could pass the run to graduate.

Gunny worked with me in the gym on our days off. He helped me increase the strength in my leg and lighten the load on my hip flexor. Jenn, with her sprinting ability, also helped me with my legs by showing me how to run more properly. With my previous boxing experience and having to do a lot of roadwork, I taught her how to breathe better, and conserve energy to help avoid the asthma attacks. It was a team effort as Gunny continued to work with me on strength, while Jenn and I would run together at night when we had day shifts.

Every evening we could, Jenn and I would go down to Long Beach, NY and run on the boardwalk instead of the hard pavement. With all the running we did daily, it was a softer surface and put less wear and tear on our legs. We would talk about everything and wound up becoming good friends. Aside from the academy, we had a lot in common as we both grew up in East Meadow, attended

THE POLICE ACADEMY

the same junior high school, and both had fathers who were retired cops.

It astounded me that we had never met before until that day on the train platform. When I had graduated 8th grade at Woodland, she was graduating from 9th grade there. Had it not been for all the fights I got into, we would've gone to East Meadow High School together. We also had mutual friends in common, and she worked at the local Friendly's restaurant as a kid. I used to go to that Friendly's all the time with my friends, and we still never met after countless opportunities to do so.

She wasn't like anyone I ever met before, and our bond continued to grow. Jenn was shy and quiet, yet very funny and quick-witted when she came out of her shell. She also had a temper and could curse like a sailor if the mood allowed it, which was very funny coming from such a cute, petite woman. I would laugh at her when the hot temper came out and she'd give me this look I can't describe. Coming from a big Irish family, she could also keep pace with me when it came to enjoying a drink or 10. Overall, Jenn was a fun person to hang out with and came from a strict family like mine.

I really liked her a lot, but there was one thing holding me back, my girlfriend. Despite the fact our relationship was toxic, I had to do the right thing. I refrained from telling Jenn how I felt as to not get her wrapped up into my drama and hurt her. Plus, with my girlfriend, even though things were bad with her and I didn't see much of a future at this point, I didn't want to hurt her either.

I felt stuck in this pattern and had passed up opportunities for good relationships throughout the years. Every time my girlfriend and I would break up, I'd date around only to go back to her. It was this never-ending cycle of toxicity and not being able to break free from someone who wasn't right for me anymore. My dad's advice about women in the NYPD didn't help either. It made me more reluctant to take a risk and leave what I had, to start a relationship with a female cop. On top of it all, my own awkwardness made me question if Jenn even liked me back. All this torture might be for nothing anyway.

It was tiring and this time was more confusing to me than any other time before. My head hit the pillow one night and I whispered to myself, praying for answers, and praying for help.

Chapter 17: Into the Dark

Thursday, August 14, 2003 was no different than any other day for us as I woke up and did my typical routine. Throughout the academy, we did a week of days and a week of 4-12's with weekends off. This was our week of days, so I rolled out of bed at 4am to drive in for the day and save some stress on my leg. It was a couple of weeks since I had dropped out of a run due to the leg, but I didn't want to take any chances.

Typically, when I drove in, everyone would pile into my car. It was a free ride for them and saved them some hassle of the train. For some reason, nobody wanted to come with me, so I drove in alone. We had a normal day at the academy and even when I offered a ride home to everyone, they all declined and decided to take the train. I shrugged my shoulders, walked to my car, and began the drive home by myself.

By the time I got to my car, got it out of the parking garage, and sat in traffic to get to the Battery Tunnel, it was a little bit after 4pm. Traffic was bad through the tunnel, but not out of the ordinary for rush hour. As traffic crawled through the exhaust fume-laden tube, the lights went off and things went dark. The lights flickered again, then went dark for good. I didn't know what was going on, but I was waiting for a wall of water and mud to kill me as we all came to a permanent stop.

Nothing happened and traffic started to slowly move again. As I got to the end of the tunnel and able to see the exit, I noticed that all the toll screens were blank, and the arms were up. Toll agents were waving everyone through slowly, and traffic was built up as far as the eye could see. Helicopters were up in the air everywhere and every electronic DOT sign was off. When I turned on the AM radio, the news was frantically talking about a major power outage in NYC and throughout the Northeast.

I couldn't get through to anyone and didn't know if my fellow classmates were ok. I was also supposed to stop at my girlfriend's house that evening to take care of the cats, because she was on a business trip. All cellphone towers were dead, and it took me over 6 hours to get home. Old-school telephone landlines were still working, so I was able to reach out to my parents and let them know I was ok. I also contacted the academy as per their policy during a major event. They told me we were being mobilized, and to be back at the academy at 5am the next morning. There was no contact with anyone else since I couldn't use the landline to call cell numbers.

As I was feeding the cats and changing out their litter box, the phone rang in the apartment. It was my girlfriend, and I told her what was going on. She got mad at me for taking so long to get to the cats. I tried explaining how bad the traffic was and why, but she didn't want to hear it. When I dropped the news on her that we were being mobilized and I had to be back at 5am to help with the blackout, she freaked out and went on an incoherent rant; all because I couldn't give her a timeline on things as far as taking care of the cats.

"What do you mean you don't know when you'll be home? Is this how it's gonna be whenever something happens at work?!" she yelled. I simply answered, "Yes, this is the way it's going to be." "Well, I don't know if I can handle this!" she exclaimed. The

Universe had opened a door for me at that very moment. Unlike years in the past, I took a deep breath, walked through the door into the unknown, and walked out. I had no idea what I was doing, but I didn't care at this point. Almost 10 years of history were gone in an instant, and we broke up for good.

While I had just ended life as I knew it relationship-wise, my classmates were stuck in NYC because they decided to take the train. They were immediately mobilized and assisted people by helping them exit the trains and subways. You'd think I was lucky to get home and be in the comfort of a house, but I roasted in the heat that night with no air conditioning. There was also a lack of sleep due to my mind racing about breaking up with my girlfriend. I would've rather been with my crew at that point.

However, something magical happened that night without me knowing it. At the same exact time I was having that argument with my girlfriend and breaking up with her, 30 miles away was Jenn. She was stuck at Penn Station, telling a mutual friend that she secretly liked me. She was sad that I had a girlfriend, so she kept her mouth shut, never saying a word. Our friend assured her that she would get us together and "talk her up" to me, but it wasn't even necessary.

The following day for me consisted of getting to the academy by car with all the traffic lights out, and cops on every corner waving me through. We gathered up at the building, then sent out on foot posts across various locations. My post was in front of the Red Lobster by Times Square, and the smell of rotting seafood was atrocious. To their credit, they were discarding the food and keeping everything clean, but we were stuck with the wafting smell of spoiled seafood on a hot summer day.

For the first time in the academy, I got a taste of how the NYPD operates under a crisis, all while being separated from my classmates. We were all scattered about due to some of us working days, some nights, and some being immediately mobilized. I didn't see anybody for the next 2 days, including Jenn. We also didn't run together that weekend since everyone was exhausted. I stayed at home that weekend, got some sleep, and licked my wounds from the breakup.

The following Monday, we were on our scheduled week of night shifts. Before class started, my friend called me over to her seat and asked very directly, "What do you think of Jenn?" while looking at my eyes to gauge a reaction. I shrugged my shoulders and just smiled at her. "You like her!" she said in an accusatory tone, "I knew it!" I proceeded to tell her what happened at my girlfriend's place on Thursday and the conversation we had. Before I even filled her in, she was already scheming on how to get Jenn and I together. "Uh huh, uh huh, mmm hmmm," she uninterestedly responded as I was telling her my story. "You have to ask her out!" she interrupted and blurted out fast.

The funny thing is, it's the last thing I remember before we started dating. Not even Jenn remembers me asking her out, our first date, or first kiss. Our friendship just slowly evolved into a relationship, with her claiming I "seduced her". A silly smile appears on her face every time she tells me that story. Regardless of how it happened or when, it was as if the blackout moved the chess pieces around for us.

It took me a while to tell Jenn about the dream I had before going into the academy, but she was the girl who gave me the pencil and called me her husband. While Jenn wasn't in my class as depicted in the dream, she was in my squad, and we all studied together after the first test. Sometimes the special dreams I had were more symbolic than direct, and this was one of them. Cosmic forces were in play here and Jenn knew it, even if she didn't know about the dream yet. Things began to move fast with us, and it didn't surprise me.

Chapter 18: The Final Test

Graduating the academy came in a series of challenges, including the final run at Floyd Bennett Field. It wasn't hot outside anymore. It was late fall/early winter, and it was very cold. In fact, near-record heat shifted to near-record cold, and we wound up with some nasty snowstorms for the winter of 2003/2004. Before all of that, we were about to face the final test to see if we were worthy.

First came the final run on a cold, windy day in November. Just as during the summer, the instructors had us sit on the tarmac and wait our turn. The wind was fierce that day, blowing from the northwest at 25 mph and gusting to 40+ mph across the open field. Temperatures that morning in the 40s felt like 30s with the wind factored in. The sun was shining like last time, but it was useless and failed to warm us up. It was close to our turn when Gunny turned to me and asked, "Are you gonna stay with me this time?" I looked at him dead in the eye and replied, "The question is, will you keep up with *me*?" He gave out this big belly laugh and said back, "All right Ben, calm down."

It was our turn to run and this time, the cold weather let us see all the way down the field without the waves of heat distorting the visibility. "I think I like not seeing the end of the course better," I nervously said to one of the other recruits. We started off and with the wind to our backs, we were flying. Breathing was easy, right leg was "all-systems go", and I kept up with Gunny the entire way. When we turned the corner to come back for the last 1/2 mile, the wind smacked us in the face as if we hit a brick wall.

We all struggled against the wind as our clothes acted like sails and slowed us down. The only one who didn't have a problem, was one of the recruits who weighed 90lbs soaking wet. He slipped through the breeze like a piece of paper held to the side and passed us as if we were standing still. Most of us passed the finish line in a large group, completing it in about 10 minutes and 30 seconds. It took us about 6 minutes to run the first mile, then 4 minutes and 30 seconds to finish it; that's how bad the wind was. Jenn finished her run also without any asthma attacks and passed, but she had challenges ahead that paled in comparison to the rest of us.

During another cycle at the range in December for more firearms training, Jenn suffered from frostbite and damaged her hands. They didn't allow gloves at the range due to them interfering with training, so we were all exposed to the elements. Her hands were so bad, they looked like that of a dead person. The academy and the doctors were skeptical if she would get to the end of the academy and graduate. She was very frustrated, in pain, and scared at the prospect of making it all this way, then not passing.

During a weekend off and close to graduation, Jenn and I had our first road trip together. We spent an overnight in Boston and had a great time, but the issue with her hands still weighed heavily on her mind. Walking outside one night back to the hotel, we stopped at a dimly lit street and talked. The one streetlight shined on her face, highlighting her breath in the cold air. Tears streamed down her face as she wept about her hands. She was in a lot of pain and things were not looking good. I gave her a hug and assured her that everything was going to be ok, but even I didn't know if they would or not.

THE FINAL TEST

I prayed that night. I prayed for her, and I prayed for us. I was fearful that she would slip through my hands, and I'd lose her if she didn't make it through the academy. I was afraid we would go our separate ways professionally, ending the relationship. When we returned from Boston, a neighbor who had connections helped Jenn get through the process, and she was allowed to graduate.

We didn't know how she wound up with frostbite so easily, but several months later, she was diagnosed with Reynaud's Syndrome, which affects the blood circulation of the hands. Years after that, we found out that the Reynaud's was Scleroderma, a very dangerous auto-immune disease. Not knowing what was in store for her yet, Jenn was ecstatic to graduate with us, and I was happy to have her there with me.

In late December of 2003, we walked down the aisles and filled the seats on the floor of Madison Square Garden. It was a sea of blue as we sat in our dress uniforms and white gloves for our parents and loved ones to see. As I sat there, I couldn't believe this journey and all the long, twisting roads it took to get me here. It took tragedy, illness, injury, disembodied voices, horrible nightmares, and the guidance of the mysterious green light. I was thankful for it all and my life was coming together.

After the graduation ceremony was done, our families went back to Long Island to celebrate together with some Italian food at our favorite restaurant. It was the first time we had our entire family together at one table. Jenn's family was very nice to me, and I knew we had something very special. You'd think that the story ended there, and whatever was guiding me had completed its mission, but the story was just getting started.

Chapter 19:
The Devil Wears Nada

After graduating, we were still attached to the police academy, before being shipped out to our assigned commands 2 weeks later. Jenn was assigned to the 102nd Precinct in Richmond Hill, Queens. I wound up being a stone's throw away at the 106th Precinct in Ozone Park/Howard Beach. I wanted to follow in my dad's footsteps and work in Brooklyn or Far Rockaway, but of course the Universe had other plans and kept me close to Jenn.

Regardless, I proudly put on my "106" collar brass for the first time and headed out for our first assignment as police officers, which was New Years Eve at Times Square. It was traditional for the summer academy class to work New Year's Eve as their first time out in the wild, and this year was no different. For months on end, instructors kept driving home into our minds, "Don't make plans on December 31st." This was because we all worked it in one capacity or another.

While we all thought we'd be working the night together, Jenn was assigned "Day Tour Barriers". "What is this shit?" I asked as most of us were expected to stand out in the 30 degree temperatures that night. She just snickered and gave me that "Ha! Ha!" look, knowing she'd be home and toasty in bed at night as the rest of us froze our balls off. Even though I would've liked her out there with us, something was probably protecting her due to her damaged hands and sensitivity to cold temperatures. Jenn was upset she didn't make plans after being told not to for all this time, so I promised to swing by after my shift to give her a New Year's kiss. She smiled and gave me an enthusiastic, "Ok!"

Her day in the city consisted of putting out barriers in 45 degree weather and setting up the holding pens for the celebration. While she was wrapping up her day, I drove into Manhattan in my personal car. I parked it as close as I could to the edge of the tow-away zone without having to worry. It was frowned upon to take our own cars to assignments while in uniform. However, being able to get out quick and get home for that kiss, was more important to me.

I climbed out of the car, no longer the Mazda since it finally died in severe cold. I walked to my post as stiff as a board due to a poor choice in undergarments. With a cold night expected, we had all ordered military-grade thermals to keep us warm. In hindsight, they didn't do shit. That was when I first learned that "military-grade" didn't equate to being superior. Not only did they not keep me warm, but they were also hard to move in. It felt as if I was trying walk through wet cement.

Before even getting to my post, I heard a chief barking orders at everyone. "Put this here! Put it back! No, put it back the other way!" he barked indecisively, as he had everyone rearranging Jenn's hard work. I was getting a firsthand look and taste of what the next 20 years would be like. I joined in to help my fellow cops move things around; then another chief walked by and asked us, "Why did you move these barriers? Who told you to do that? Put it back!" I looked at the senior officer in charge of babysitting us newbies on our posts and he said, "Welcome to the NYPD," while rolling his eyes.

As partygoers began to trickle into the holding pens, the sergeant came by to give us our assigned posts. We stood around for a few more minutes, bullshitting about which precincts we were going to after training. "106? What the fuck is that?!" one of my buddies taunted me as he stood there proudly with his "75" collar brass on. "You must've had *some* phone call," he added. In reality, I had no phone calls or connections. It was a roll of the dice. Everyone my dad knew was either long-retired or dead. A lieutenant walked by and ordered us to go to our assigned pens, seemingly annoyed at the banter.

Nighttime fell as did the temperatures, but things were about to get a little warmer. I turned around to scan my pen and made sure everyone was behaving. In the front row was this beautiful woman with black hair, blue eyes, red lipstick, and a big smile. She stood out as she was on another level beauty-wise compared to most ladies you'd normally see in public. Dressed in a white fur coat and fur hat, it didn't look like she had anything on underneath.

Every time I went to look at the pen and the crowd, she was up against the barrier, staring directly at me. I tried not to make eye contact, but I could only ignore her so many times before it looked rude. Our eyes met and she smiled while mouthing "Hi" at me. I glanced for a second and gestured "Hi" back with a shy wave of my hand. "What are you doing?" I asked myself. "You're a New York City cop. Stop being a wuss and go talk to her," as the conversation continued in my head while she stared at me.

I walked over and we started talking. Aside from her beauty, she was very nice to me and helped me keep my mind occupied from being so damn cold. As to not get in trouble or look like I wasn't doing my job, I'd scan my pen, talk to her, take a break, then look around at the other pens. "Psssst!" one of my academy-mates said loudly while waving me over. "Pssssssst!" he looked at me again with big eyes in excitement while waving me over again.

"What!" I yelled back to him. "Come here for a second!" he replied while trying to whisper but not whispering at all.

I walked over and with this weird look on his face, he asked, "Do you know who that is?" "No?" I replied in a semi-confused way. He proceeded to yell the name of a celebrity. I said, "No way it's her!" while brushing him off. He took my head with his hands, physically turning it towards her, and said, "Look at her!" I glanced over at her as she stood there, reapplying her lipstick while looking around for me. "She wants you, dude!" my buddy said with a goofy smile, while shoving me to walk back to the pen.

The walk back to her felt no different than the long walk to the ring during the Golden Gloves. My hands got clammy in the winter gloves, and I felt nauseous. "Get yourself together, Ben," I said to myself as she looked at me demurely and smiled. "Hey," I said to her. "Hey," she said back. "What were you and your friend talking about?" she asked with another smile. "Nothing," I replied as I scanned around, pretending to do my job.

She tapped me on my shoulder to get my attention and on the inside I jumped. On the outside though, I turned around and pretended as if I were cool. "What are you doing after your shift? Would you like to come back to my place?" she asked directly. I looked at her beautiful face, sparkling eyes, and up and down at the fur coat seemingly hiding a naked body underneath. I couldn't hear any sound in a sea of millions of people. It was just her and I at that very moment.

"I'm sorry, I can't. I'm seeing someone," I apologetically said to her while crying in agony on the inside. "Okayyyyyy?" she replied in shock that somebody turned her down. The music and noise got loud again as the moment passed, and we were sucked back into reality. I screamed over the noise and said to her, "I'm sorry! I promised her a New Year's kiss tonight when I get home!" The beautiful celebrity got quiet, things got awkward, and she slipped back into the crowd as the ball dropped. It was one of the craziest moments in my life and nobody saw it, or at least I thought so.

I drove home that night, talking to myself, and hitting the steering wheel with my palm. I felt like an idiot and proud of myself at the same time. I had turned down the ultimate temptation, the story of a lifetime, and a night with a beautiful celebrity. Me, a lowly city cop, had a one-in-a-million chance, and I passed it up. I drove back to East Meadow to give Jenn the most passionate kiss I could. I pulled up to the house at 2am, walked up to the front door, knocked gently, and nobody answered. There was no New Year's kiss that night; she had fallen asleep.

The next day at the academy I hated myself. Although I did the right thing, I turned down the "road to infamy" for a New Year's kiss that never happened. "Nobody would've known," I said to myself, and I was wrong. Everyone on my post that night knew what happened. They were all watching me as if it were spectator sport, laughing at me when I turned her down. Word got around and it eventually got back to Jenn. The Devil wore nada that night and I passed a very hard test. Had I gone down that path, Jenn would've found out, and nothing I have today would exist.

When I had the celebrity actress in my pen that night, a chief came up to me with a big smile and said, "It's all downhill from here, kid! Ya peaked early in your career." Just like when he had us rearrange all those barriers for no apparent reason, he was wrong.

PART IV

Chapter 20: Hot Cocoa

New Year's Eve and our brief 2 week introduction to the streets were over. It was time to head to our prospective precincts and begin our lives as cops for real. There was no "safety net" anymore as the realities and dangers of being a cop hit with blunt force. For Jenn, the 102nd Precinct was an "impact zone" where all the rookies stood on foot posts in the frigid cold along Jamaica Ave.

For me, the 106th Precinct only got 4 cops out of the academy, and they were desperate for manpower. There was no real field training for the most part as it was very short, and they needed us out there. Basically, we were handed a radio, keys to an RMP, and a map of the precinct. The desk sergeant grumbled to us rookies, "Get the fuck out of my face and answer some jobs!" We were thrown into the fire and handled countless accidents, domestic disputes, EDPs (emotionally disturbed persons) and other calls in a short time.

With my dad's help, I was already semi-prepared and had a good foundation in terms of what to expect/how to conduct myself. It was also time to look for a new place to live, fulfilling a promise to move back out after graduating the academy. Although I knew I had to leave my parents and never wanted to be back there in the first place, trying to find an apartment and figuring out how to afford it on this new salary, was a daunting task while juggling a new life on patrol.

Meanwhile, it was hard to get any quality time with Jenn since she worked a different schedule and had different days off. The only way to get some real time with her was to wait for my days off to "swing" into hers. I could also sneak over to the 102nd Precinct after my shift to see her on post. It was risky as we could both get in trouble, but she was struggling out in the frigid cold with her Reynaud's-inflicted hands. No gloves, no hand warmers, no thermals, and no jacket would keep her hands from turning blue, purple, and a waxy white. It continued to be a very painful ordeal for her, so I did what I could to help.

Almost every night I'd wait for the supervisors to leave, roll up in my car, and let her sit inside with the heat blasting. I'd also bring her a cup of hot cocoa every night so that she can warm up internally and help warmer blood flow to her hands. Had we gotten caught, we would've surely both received a "command discipline" and have vacation time taken away from us. It didn't matter to me. Her health was the most important thing, and I wanted to see her thrive.

This went on for a few months before the temperatures started to moderate, and we never got caught. One day while sitting in the car, I asked her if she wanted to look for a place together and move in with me. There was no hesitation on her part, and we began looking for places whenever we had a day off together. Eventually, we found an upstairs apartment in Long Beach. It wound up being just 2 blocks away from the boardwalk we used to run on together as friends.

After a few months, Jenn got sent to the 107th Precinct which covered Fresh Meadows, parts of Flushing, and Jamaica Estates. It was time for her to join patrol, and she wound up in my squad. This meant she had the same days off and same shift, affording us more time together. On a cold day during late winter, we moved into the Long Beach apartment and started the next chapter of our lives.

Jenn got nervous about moving in with me knowing what it was like to live with boys. She had 2 younger brothers who always made a mess. To her relief, I wasn't a messy person and was already used to living on my own or with another girl. We spent the next 2 weeks setting up our new home, and she was pleasantly surprised at how easy it was. It's hard to explain, but everything just flowed perfectly, and we were a good couple.

Even if it seemed quick, I knew what I wanted in life, and knew she was the one for me. I had a talk with my parents, and it went much smoother than I thought. Because it was so soon, I thought I'd catch a hard time from them. The next step was a tougher challenge in my eyes, and I expected some resistance.

I went over to her parent's house to ask Jenn's dad permission to marry her. He was a very strict man and had a Suffolk Highway Patrol demeanor to him. There were other issues too as she was Roman Catholic and I was Jewish. It didn't matter to me, but I wasn't sure if it mattered to them as crucifixes hung on the walls throughout the house, and they went to Church every Sunday.

When I knocked on the door, Jenn's mom and one of her younger brothers already knew why I was there. As I sat down in the dining room to have a very serious talk with her dad, her mom disappeared to give us privacy. Meanwhile, Jenn's brother was pacing back and forth in the living room, laughing like "Beavis & Butthead". I wanted to die as I was trying to keep a straight face, all while talking to this man looking at me with a stone-cold face. After I finally got it out and said what needed to be said, his demeanor changed. He said with a smile and a shrug, "Well she's the one who's gotta say yes."

I was relieved and shook his hand. Meanwhile, Jenn's brother was still pacing back and forth, laughing like a moron. Jenn's mom gave me a hug and asked me when I planned to propose. The plan was to do it in April during a birthday trip to Key West, but a terrorist threat a week later made for enhanced security at the airport. I was afraid I'd get stopped at the security kiosk with the ring in my pocket, forcing me to propose right there like an idiot in front of strangers. I wanted to be in a *different* place and be an idiot in front of *different* strangers. On a day off together in March, I got down on one knee and proposed to Jenn in our apartment due to the circumstances. Before she even saw the ring, she said yes and wrapped her arms around me. Afterwards, I put my Grandma Harriet's engagement ring on her finger, and she started crying because of how beautiful it was.

Everything was coming together for Jenn as she spent the next 6 years or so in the 107th Precinct. As for me, there were some big changes coming, and the long, twisting road towards a miracle continued.

Chapter 21: Snake in the Grass

As with any NYPD rookie cop, life was not easy as there were big adjustments. The learning curve is tremendous, and you also must gain the trust of your fellow cops. Socially there are big adjustments as well. Non-police friends see changes taking place from the effects of the schedule, the streets, and the mentality needed to cope with the stresses. With the help of my dad, the learning curve was slightly less, and he taught me not to let the job "define" me.

We had many talks along the way, including the importance of doing my job and going home to Jenn every night. He didn't want me getting wrapped up in the "4 to 4" party mentality of starting my shift at 4pm, then going out drinking till 4am after work. It is the ruiner of marriages, and he wanted to show me how to keep things stable at home. He also taught me not to bring the job home. This meant when the uniform went into the locker at the end of the night, you left everything at work. You never take a bad day out on your loved ones.

One winter night when Jenn and I were over for dinner, my dad stepped outside for a cigarette and asked me to come out with him. The sky was crystal clear, and the stars shined as bright as the icicles hanging off the house from a previous snowstorm. "So now that you've had a couple of months on patrol, what do you think you want to do with your career?" my dad asked. "It's too early for that, dad. Where am I going?" I replied.

"No, no, I mean in the future. Now that you see what it's like, where do you see your career going?" he asked with a look on his face as if I misunderstood him. I thought about it for a minute, looked at him, and said as if I were a kid asking Santa for a gift, "I either wanna be a detective, or get into something so big, they ask me where I wanna go, and I'd pick the Harbor Unit." He looked at me, put his hands up as if trying to slow me down, and said, "Woah, woah, woah, let's not get ahead of ourselves. Getting into something so big and being asked where you wanna go, is a one-in-a-million shot." I looked at him and whimsically replied while shrugging my shoulders, "Well, those are the two things." He chuckled and we went back into the house to warm up.

Following his advice was easy and even though he retired in 1986, the rules still applied. The only thing different was the technology, but human nature and the department hadn't changed. Running from call to call made the nights go faster, and I got used to the paperwork very quickly. While the 106th Precinct wasn't a notoriously violent place, we had many domestic disputes, accidents, DOAs, EDPs, and other strange things. It was here where I had my first brush with the paranormal while in uniform.

It was still wintertime when we got a call for a burglary in progress. The radio gave out a tone, then central dispatch gave out the job. We all backed each other up and arrived at the residence together. A lady came out of the house in her bathrobe screaming, "There's someone upstairs! There's someone in my house! I heard the footsteps!" We calmed her down and had her wait outside while we went in. The sergeant took the lead with his driver, since the rest of us were either newbies or from the previous academy class.

SNAKE IN THE GRASS

We followed him through the half-opened door with our hands on our guns and still in their holsters. The sergeant had his gun out since he was the point-man, and we began to go through the house slowly. As we cleared the first floor, we heard footsteps above us. He turned around to us with big eyes and put his fingers on his lips as if to tell us, "Shut the fuck up!" We weren't talking though, and I almost burst out laughing. The sergeant went up the wood stairs, trying not to make creaking sounds, and we followed him up.

When we got to the landing and looked down the hallway, there was nothing. It was dead silent, so we stood there quietly to listen for anything. Suddenly the first door on the right slammed shut with such force, it shook the wall. The sergeant rushed to the door, kicked it in, and entered the room sweeping the area with his gun. We followed him in and there was nothing. Confusion set in as we checked under the bed, the closet, and to see if he went out of the window. The window was locked from the inside, and nothing was there.

All the windows upstairs were closed, so wind couldn't have slammed the door, and it was a calm night anyway. We all hurried out of the house, passing the lady in her bathrobe. The sergeant said while looking back, "Nothing here ma'am!" and we peeled away. We all met up in the parking lot of a convenience store after and nervously laughed about what just happened. The story went around for a couple of weeks, and everyone was asking us about it. It was a strange but funny incident. I thought it was a bonding moment too, but everything was about to fall apart fast.

Come early spring, I was doing patrol with one of the other rookies. We received a call for a snake on somebody's front lawn. We both looked at each other, shaking our heads as if the call was probably bullshit; especially since there's not much wildlife in the Ozone Park area. When we got to the call and walked up to the house, a woman pointed to an area in the grass where she saw the snake. We walked over and low and behold, there was a small snake curled up in a ball. "Call the sergeant," I said to my partner since it didn't look like anything typical for the area.

The sergeant pulled up with his driver. They gave us the same look as my partner and I did to each other initially. I pointed out where the snake was and said to the sergeant, "I think we need to call ESU (Emergency Services) on this one." His driver scoffed at me and said, "It's just a garter snake," while walking over to pick it up. I ran to intercept him and physically pushed him out of the way. He stumbled, caught his balance, and yelled, "What the fuck is wrong with you?! Who do you think you are?!" I pointed out to him that it wasn't a garter snake.

The other cops on scene had to separate us, and things almost got physical because he was offended that I pushed him. As we were in each other's face, the sergeant walked over, looked at the snake, and went over the radio, "Central, can you have ESU respond to my location for a snake? We can't identify what it is." His driver, red-faced and breathing heavily, walked away in a huff, and sat up against the sergeant's RMP. I explained to the sergeant that it looked as if the snake had venom glands on it, and that it didn't have any coloring I've ever seen before.

We waited around for ESU Truck 9 to swing by. They safely corralled the snake into a spackle bucket. One of the officers quickly covered it, and we were told to drop it off at Brooklyn Animal Control. When we dropped it off, the employees identified it as a Gaboon Viper, one of the most venomous snakes in the world. We have no idea how it got there, but what I do know is that I saved the cop's life by shoving him out of the way. We found out later that the Bronx Zoo didn't have the anti-venom for a Gaboon Viper at the time.

When we told the sergeant what it was, he couldn't believe it. As far as his driver was concerned, he didn't care that I saved him;

he was still pissed that I shoved him. Unfortunately, he was part of the clique that "ran" the precinct, and now my name was mud. For the next few months, they ostracized me and did everything they could to make my life miserable. It was hard to drive to work every day. I had to watch my back more from my fellow cops, than I did from the criminals on the streets.

In late April, all the rookies who went to the 106th Precinct, including myself, were notified that we were taking part in the "Summer Detail" at the 100th Precinct in Rockaway Beach. The timing couldn't have been any better. It offered me a temporary escape from the small group of assholes I had to deal with. I hoped that it would allow a "cooling off" period and they would forget what happened. It also gave me some comfort that it was a "homecoming" of sorts as my dad was a rookie in the 100th Precinct. He was there for a short time before being sent to the 73rd Precinct in Brooklyn for half of his career.

While it technically wasn't Far Rockaway where my family came from, I still knew the area well and was looking forward to a change of scenery. Polo shirts, shorts, sunblock, the boardwalk, and ladies in bikinis were calling my name, but it never happened that way.

Chapter 22:
I Know That Name

L ate May of 2004 arrived and I walked into the 100th Precinct for the first time. A sea of rookies filled the precinct floor in front of the desk sergeant. We eagerly awaited information on what our assignments would be. Just as years in the past, they pulled 4 rookies from each precinct across the borough of Queens South, but Jenn was not one of them. I was alone of sorts on this venture. There were a few familiar faces there from the academy, and one of them was in my company with Gunny.

My friend John was permanently assigned there, but he had nothing to do with the summer detail. I thought it would be a long summer without seeing him much. Regardless, I was looking forward to working on my tan while on the boardwalk. "Reiver! I know that name!" a voice yelled out as I turned to follow my fellow rookies towards the muster room. I turned back around to look where the voice came from, and it was a lieutenant behind the precinct desk. He waved me over and I stood in front of him, posed in a semi-attention stance.

"Relax, kid!" he motioned with his hands, "Do you have family on the job?" I replied, "My dad, but he retired a long time ago out of the 101." His eyes grew big, and he smiled. "Sam Reiver. You're Sam's son?" he asked. I nodded my head yes and he pounded the desk with glee. "Your dad was my training officer when I was a rookie in the 101. If you're anything like him, you're staying here," he said. I had no idea what was going on as I never encountered or expected to encounter anyone who knew my dad.

For the next hour I stood there as he proceeded to tell me stories about my dad, and how crazy he was. In the same respect, he told me how even keeled my dad was unless someone tried something on him. "Man oh man your dad was a good cop," he said while smiling. I turned my head towards the muster room to see what the other rookies were doing. The Lieutenant yelled "Hey!" to get my attention again. He said, "Don't worry about them, kid. You're backfilling patrol. I wanna see what you got."

While I was happy to hear stories about my dad, I felt deflated there for a moment since I would not be on the boardwalk having fun. It was customary for the 100th Precinct to keep one rookie every year from the summer detail, and the Lieutenant wanted to see if I was the one. The only way to do that was to do patrol with him and the other guys on his shift. It also meant that I was at mercy of the other bosses. I was a newbie all over again, because nobody had a clue who I was.

The one bright spot out of this new development was that I got to stay in my squad from when I was on patrol in the 106th Precinct. The guys on the boardwalk had steady days off and rotating shifts. With me sticking to my previous schedule, Jenn and I still had the same days off, and were able to continue to plan our wedding. My dad was also excited for me, and he gave me his original "100" collar brass that were silver in color. I stood out from everyone else because collar brass hadn't been silver since the late 1960s/early 1970s. This is when I had the "pleasure" of meeting the other lieutenant.

"Officer Reeever," he said to me with a nasally robotic voice as if to have me approach the desk. I walked up and corrected him,

"It's Reiver (Rye-ver), sir." He looked at me with his dark beady eyes and asked, "Officer Reeever, why do you have silver collar brass on?" I replied, "They're my dad's from when he was a rookie here and he gave them to me." "Those are unauthorized," he replied in a louder and more monotone robotic voice. While I respected the rank, I automatically lost respect for this guy and knew what type of boss he was for giving me a hard time about such a trivial thing.

Knowing I had the other lieutenant's back and the NYPD being very big on tradition, I looked him dead in the eye and replied, "They're my dad's, I'm not taking them off." His eyes got big, and he sank back into his seat like a coward, not saying another word. The "Robot" would wind up being a thorn in my side for a long time, but for the moment, he left me alone as the other lieutenant oversaw me officially.

I settled into patrol rather nicely, listening to more stories about my dad while driving the lieutenant around for the first couple of weeks. There was no need for a map to the precinct since I already knew the area fairly well. He was excited to have me there and had high hopes for me. "I see you have your dad's instincts," he enthusiastically stated, while watching me point out all the suspicious activity and making some good stops. "Eventually, we're gonna pair you up with someone and put you guys out there alone," he said confidently.

I still missed the boardwalk. Watching those guys have fun, when all we could do is take a quick ride up there with the RMP, gave me a sinking feeling. "I'm missing out," I used to say to myself as I was stuck answering jobs on the radio. The other rookies got to stare at girls in bikinis all day and got glorious tans. However, the Universe had other plans for me, and I was about to get a glimpse of it with a couple of odd coincidences. The lieutenant wanted me to learn every aspect of the 100th Precinct, so the following week he put me with the Housing guys.

The NYPD had their own Housing Unit, but they didn't cover the housing projects in the Rockaways anymore. Because of this, both the 101st and the 100th Precinct had their own cops covering it. The lieutenant wanted to make sure I could handle the task, so he introduced me to the Housing sergeant. He was one of those crazy, old-school, street crime cops, who could just look at someone and point out who had a gun on them. Being a master at his craft, everyone looked to him for guidance. He took me under his wing for the week and showed me all the ins-and-outs of housing.

Throughout that period, we got to talking and found out a lot about one other. While the sergeant didn't compete like I did, he was also a boxer and personally knew my old trainer, Al Gavin. During the summer, Al passed away, and the sergeant let me attend his wake when I was scheduled to work. We knew some of the same people growing up and the sergeant had a deep respect for me. In an even stranger twist, a few years later he attended my ex-girlfriend's wedding because she married someone he knew.

Nonetheless, the chess pieces were on the move again and beyond my control. With each day passing, they grew happier with my work ethic and instincts. When the lieutenant needed a condition taken care of, he'd send me out on a foot post to investigate it. If the Housing sergeant knew something was about to become physical, he'd give me a call knowing he'd have a 2nd person there with him who could fight if need be. Overall, I was learning a lot more in the 100th than I ever could in the 106th Precinct. While the 100th Precinct had a reputation around the city for being a "slow house", the summer was busy, and it was much busier than Ozone Park/Howard Beach. Even though things were going well, there were still rookie mistakes to be made.

I KNOW THAT NAME

One day out on patrol, I was partnered with another new guy when we got hit by a band of slow-moving thunderstorms. It was a dreary day, and the rain just kept coming as the storms parked themselves across the south shore of New York City. Rain, thunder, and wind continued for hours on end, and the precinct was dead activity-wise on the radio. We decided to take the car up onto the boardwalk and enjoy the silence since there were no beachgoers.

With the wind picking up and the wet wood of the boardwalk providing a slippery surface, the RMP started to drift a little bit as the side of the car began acting like a kite in the wind. "We should get off of the boardwalk," I said to my partner. He agreed and we got off at the end of it along the Beach 120 streets. We went up the block and decided to make a right onto Rockaway Beach Boulevard. I saw something strange coming down the street from west to east. "What's that?" I asked my partner. "Go, go, go!" he exclaimed. It was a wall of water coming down the street in the form of a flash flood.

I had nowhere to go. There was a car in front of me blocking the intersection. I hit reverse as if to back up and go around him, but it was too late. The wall of water hit the car and carried us down the boulevard. It was about 2 feet of water, just enough to lift the car, float us down towards the precinct, and destroy it. You could smell the sizzling electronics regardless of me turning the car off at some point. One of the sergeants had to come out and rescue us in one of the trucks, and he was pissed!

We spent the next 2 weeks on foot posts in the worst areas of the precinct as punishment. However, I wound up making a few good arrests on my post, so I was back in the good graces of the supervisors. That one sergeant busted my balls about it for months, but he was just angry at the world. With multiple divorces under his wing, and his paycheck reduced to pennies due to child support, he had to find someone else to be angry at other than himself.

The summer flew by and overall, it was a success. I had earned my keep at the 100th Precinct and they wanted me to stay. However, I had to go back to my old command first, since this was just a temporary assignment. During the summer, Jenn and I were able to solidify our wedding plans. We were set to get married on June 26th the following year. It wasn't until writing this book that I realized the significance of the date. June 26th was the same day I received the phone call in Vegas that I was in the academy. It was the only Sunday available in the late spring/early summer when we were booking the wedding.

There were also more oddities along the way, one of which I found out after returning to the 100th Precinct. Upon returning, I partnered up with my old academy-mate, John. We were assigned steady sector Adam/Boy for the most part, which covered the Hammel Houses. While browsing online at home one day, I decided to check out my friend Ezra's memorial page. September 11th was on my mind, and I was thinking back at all the things that brought me to this point. I saw in the comments that Ezra had spent his childhood in the Hammel Houses, born and raised in Rockaway Beach.

I was patrolling the streets he grew up on, brought here to protect his neighborhood. Everything was coming together, and I was about to marry the woman sent to me during this whole crazy journey.

Chapter 23: Interfaith Rabbi

Throughout the relationship and engagement, our different religions were never an issue between Jenn and I. We both believed in God, having similar views about the Church and Synagogue based on our experiences in the past. That being said, she offered to convert to Judaism, and I refused to allow that. I was honored, but it was equally important to me that she kept her own identity. It was out of respect for her family and her birthright. Jenn taking my name was enough in my eyes, and she had to keep something of her own.

Between the two of us, we decided to keep things neutral and have a non-religious ceremony to try and make everyone happy. It was a decision that both sets of parents disagreed on, so we tried to seek out priests and rabbis who would work together at the ceremony. We searched around to no avail, but I came across a rabbi who specialized in conducting interfaith marriages. I arranged a meeting with him to discuss how the ceremony would go, just to make sure it was what we were looking for. He was a very soft-spoken man, and we liked what he was telling us, so we hired him.

Meanwhile, the final touches were being made for the rest of the wedding. At the place we moved to in Long Beach, the landlord downstairs had a daughter who had just started a wedding cake business in the city. She was so new, this would've been her 7th or so cake, and she was still baking everything out of her house. We took a drive out to Staten Island, and she was a lovely woman. We had a cake design in mind that I had come up with and sketched out for her. When she said she could do it, we hired her on the spot. Years later, she became so well-known, her cakes were being used for events held by Fortune 500 companies. What is even crazier, was that my design wound being her #1 requested cake at weddings.

If our parents wanted the big New York wedding instead of the small one we had in mind, the deal was that Jenn would get the fancy cake, and I can hire a band. My family was a musical one, and although I couldn't play an instrument for the life of me, I could sing and had a good ear for music. I already had a band in mind and hired them after Jenn got to hear them play at an event. During the planning, I secretly made a deal to sing a few songs with them without Jenn knowing. I'd slip off to practice with them a few nights, and the stage was set for a beautiful wedding.

As with most weddings, nothing ever goes as planned. For us, it went very smoothly except for 2 things. The day of our wedding wound up being one of the hottest days of the year, if not the hottest. We didn't have a particularly hot summer overall, but on this day during early summer, the sun decided to rest itself on the earth's surface. Without a cloud in the sky and no wind, temperatures reached into the mid 90s to scorch everything.

Wedding guests wilted in the heat outside even though we handed out parasols for the ladies. The dresses were too heavy for the heat, and things were unbearable for many during the outdoor ceremony. As for me, the wool suit trained me well. With no alcohol in my body, I held up alright in my black tuxedo considering it felt like a pizza oven outside. The guests took their seats, the interfaith rabbi took his spot, and I walked up the aisle.

INTERFAITH RABBI

When Jenn entered the picture and started walking down the aisle towards me, the past 29 years came rushing back. Everything that brought me to this moment, the chance encounters, the coincidences, the setbacks, the voices, and the green light, all rushed through my mind.

Next thing I knew, Jenn was standing in front of me, and the rabbi roared like a lion with a loud prayer in Hebrew. I was immediately brought back into my body and mortified as I thought it was going to be more of a low-key interfaith ceremony. I looked at him as he had his eyes closed and arms reaching towards the sky. Then I looked at Jenn and we both gave each other an uncomfortable smile; trying not to make each other laugh during the theatrics. Before you knew it, we exchanged vows, rings, kissed, and the ceremony was over.

The first thing I did was go over to Jenn's parents and apologize for the ceremony being less interfaith than we thought it would be. They were completely fine with it since they wanted the ceremony to have more of a religious tone anyway. I breathed a sigh of relief. With the weight lifted off my shoulders, it was party time, and it was a grand old party. Everyone had a great time, and it was one of those weddings that people still talk about to this day.

The food was great, the cake was amazing, and the band kicked ass. Jenn and I had our first dance to "We Belong Together" by Robert & Johnny. It felt as if the song went on forever as we danced closely for everyone to watch. It truly felt like heaven for a moment; then I broke off to sing with the band as they switched the pace up. Nobody knew what I had planned, and everyone was in shock when I hit the stage. Very few people knew I could sing. The crowd went wild on the dance floor as I sang "Splish Splash" by Bobby Darin and "Twistin' the Night Away" by Sam Cooke.

It was a great day in our lives, and the honeymoon was incredible. The entire moment was a great reprieve from the realities of being an NYPD couple. However, reality was waiting for me in strange form once we broke out of the protective cocoon of wedding cake, impromptu singing cameos, and the beauty of Hawaii.

Chapter 24: Area 100

Jenn and I settled into married life pretty easily, but I had to work on my other "marriage" now that it was time to resume patrol. My partner John and I were a good team together, and we had a lot of fun. The two of us were completely different personality-wise, but it worked because we balanced each other out. He was the "schmoozer" and good at talking to the bosses, smoothing things over, and keeping things light. I was the no-nonsense cop when things got physical and beyond the point of smoothing anything over. We complemented each other well, and it kept us out of trouble aside from the occasional run-in with Lieutenant Robot.

One of my favorite things to do with John was go to "Critical Response" with him when given the opportunity. Critical Response was a function of our counter-terrorism operations in the NYPD. We would caravan together in our RMPs, broken down by borough, and go to designated locations they deemed "soft targets" at risk for terrorist activity. While there was work to be done, there was nothing like taking a break from regular patrol in the 100th Precinct. It was fun being part of the tourist attractions in Manhattan and having a nice cigar while out on post. Smoking in uniform was against regulations, but nobody cared or ever gave us a hard time. John and I would stand on post, bullshit with each other, and daydream about going to the Harbor Unit one day. We'd think up ridiculous scenarios that would get us off patrol, since we both loved the water.

Once we were done with Critical Response for the night and crossed the bridge from Brooklyn to Queens, it was back to reality. Rockaway was a strange place and had several nicknames such as "Rockapulco", "Fort Zero", and "The Land That Time Forgot". In retrospect, although nobody used this name, it'll always be "Area 100" (a play on Area 51) to me due to all the strange happenings. The precinct always had a weird vibe to me, with EDPs walking around everywhere in a trance.

There were a lot of old homes that were designated to take care of psych patients, and they would just let them roam free like Iberico Ham. Most of them were harmless, but occasionally things would get tough. We'd get stuck in the hospital sometimes; watching them until they went nighty-night courtesy of a "B52" injection. With all the strange energy, old homes, and dilapidated buildings, hauntings were widespread in particular spots. That being said, my first brush in Rockaway wasn't with any spirits, it was with "aliens".

We got a call one night for a water rescue near the Belle Harbor area of Rockaway. A caller down on the beach saw what they thought was a distress flare. While it was the Harbor Unit's job to physically go out and respond to where someone was in distress, it was our responsibility to try and assess the situation from land since our precinct covered the beach. When we got there, FDNY and EMTs were already on scene in case it was something at the shore. A crowd of people were there as well, looking out into the dark, still waters.

We waited several minutes and watched to no avail. The caller was adamant that they saw something, so we gave it a few more minutes. Just as we began walking back to the RMP and "close the job" out, we heard someone yell, "There it is again!" We turned around and walked back up to the beach entrance. There was a red light in the sky in the same general direction as the boat anchorage. This area is where ships wait to get clearance into NYC Harbor. It could've been a flare, so we waited for it to drop and fizzle out. The shimmering metallic red light remained in the same position for about 10 minutes.

One of the guys on scene who worked in the beach detail, walked back to his RMP and got binoculars. He came back, took a look, and his hands started shaking. "Hey Ben, check this out," he said while handing me the binoculars. I went to take a look, and it was a disc on a 45 degree angle that was red and orange like hot lava. There were also these tiny super-bright white and blue lights running down the middle of it. We started passing around the binoculars for everyone to take a look. They were all "oooh'ing" and "ahhh'ing" as we were trying to figure out what to say on the radio.

The light began to flicker and shake violently before rising further away from the horizon. After that, it did a little "dance" to the east and started changing color, then "Zip!" It flashed across the sky like a shooting star westward towards New Jersey before disappearing. Everyone did a collective "Woah!" and gasped before going back inside as if nothing happened. It was the strangest reaction I've ever seen to something like that, and almost as if they were used to it.

The sergeant went over the air on his radio and told central dispatch that it was an aircraft that took off and disappeared. Lieutenant Robot was also there on the scene, and I said to him, "Maybe they're here to take you home." He replied, "Heh, Heh, Heh," in his typical monotone voice. We all burst out laughing and left the scene. The following day, the precinct was crawling with press wanting to know what happened. We were instructed not to talk to anyone, but one of the local papers already knew because neighbors were talking. They ran a story which quickly disappeared, and that was it for the aliens.

I don't remember if John was there or not for that one, but we always seemed to miss each other's good stuff when either of us were on vacation. Regardless, things were going well until he met a woman down in Florida on one of his trips. He fell head-over-heels in love with her and was thinking about leaving the NYPD for Florida. His mind became distracted, and we fell out of sync on the road. When he finally decided to take the plunge and move, John and I fought like cats and dogs.

I was concerned about him and thought he was making a bad decision. My gut feeling and intuition were going crazy, and it seemed all wrong to me. He took it as if I wasn't in his corner, but I was. I felt that the risk outweighed the reward and that this was going to end badly. I learned a very valuable lesson at that moment, and it brought me back to when I used my abilities to try and get my ex-girlfriend back in 10th grade. Sometimes people must make their own mistakes, and you can't save everyone. He wound up leaving and moving down there for her.

Several years later we patched things up and he realized that I was just trying to help him, but my partner was gone, and I was left in limbo. When you're on patrol and have no partner, you get "farmed out" for everything. You spend time in the hospital watching EDPs, get sent to Critical Response with strange people, put on foot posts, and get sent out on patrol with cops whom nobody wants to work with. You might even *be* the guy nobody wants to work with, and it's a strange position to be in overall.

Eventually I partnered up with someone when *their* partner retired, but it was never the same as what I had with John. Regardless, there were weird times ahead and more strange stories. My dad had warned me not to bring anything home, and leave the stresses of the job in my locker at the end of the night; but what if something follows you home without your permission? Working patrol in Rockaway was about to take a dark turn, and there was nothing I could do about it.

Every so often, we'd get a 911 call from a disconnected line, and it was an elderly lady calling for help. It always came back to the 3rd floor of the old Neponsit Beach Hospital by Riis Park. Since I had more time on the job at this point and my partner had more experience, we would cover that area occasionally. There was nothing to investigate, since the building was abandoned and nobody was in there. The hospital itself was originally a tuberculosis sanatorium for children. It later became an old age home before being shut down.

It was rumored to be haunted, and kids in the area would test their courage by going in there to explore the area. An active security booth remained at the location due to parts of the grounds still being active electricity-wise. The kids would go in, security would call 911, and they would run out before the police got there. It was a game of "cat and mouse" that went on for generations of cops and local kids. The kids won every time, and we were tired of wasting our time driving out there for nothing.

One night we got a call to the hospital, and we happened to be on Beach 129th street getting food. That put us only a few minutes away, and the security guard said that the kids were still on the premises. We made our way over there and the anti-crime sergeant met us with his guys. The guard let us in and said he didn't see anyone come out, so we walked to the door and quietly made our way in. The sergeant led the way and peeked into the dark, dusty environment. For the first time ever, we found ourselves walking through the building.

As soon as we walked in, we heard footsteps and voices upstairs. We had to be careful though and watch our step, so we proceeded slowly. Try and picture your worst nightmare and this was worse scenery-wise. Lead paint peeled from the walls, broken glass from old fluorescent lightbulbs crunched as we walked, and old hospital beds with stained mattresses were strewn everywhere across each hallway. We continued to walk through the halls slowly so that we didn't get cut on anything and wind up with tetanus. "Did you hear that?" the sergeant asked. "Hear what?" my partner replied. I heard something, but it wasn't clear.

We stopped moving, stayed in one spot, and moved our flashlights around so that we could see in the pitch black. "Did you hear that?" I asked my partner. "No, hear what?" they replied. "That!" I whispered loudly. They shrugged their shoulders, and we continued slowly down the hallway. Suddenly, we all heard footsteps running away from us down the hallway. We shined our lights in that direction and there was nothing. You could then hear the footsteps going up the stairway toward the 3rd floor.

"Shit, shit!" the anti-crime sergeant exclaimed. "You guys take that set of stairs," as he pointed back where we came from. "We'll take these stairs," the sergeant pointed towards where we heard the footsteps go. We went towards the first set of stairs and headed up to the 3rd floor. When we got to the top and shined the lights down the dilapidated hallway, we saw the sergeant and his guys reach the top. Between the two groups and in the center of the hallway, there was a room with a light on. We slowly made our way over to the room and looked in.

The room was immaculate as if we stepped back in time. The floors were cleaned and waxed, with a black and white checkerboard pattern. It was freshly painted, and the bed was neatly made. Beyond the entry line of the room, dust and debris filled the hallway. However, there was not one speck of dust in the room, no rust on the metal-tubing furniture, and a clipboard hung from a rack with fresh paper. It was impossible that this room could exist in the environment we were in.

We stepped away from the room as our gut feelings all told us not to go in; then we heard laughing and more footsteps. This time, the footsteps were only 5 feet away or so and moving away from us again. I heard voices but couldn't make out what they were saying. It was as if someone was dialing an old radio too quickly to hear the words. After another round of footsteps, I said to my partner, "I'm leaving, let's go." I left ahead of them and when I got to the first floor, I heard footsteps coming down the stairs towards me.

I thought it was my partner and the other guys coming down, but the sound faded away as the steps got closer. It was time for me to walk out, so I waited outside for my partner and the rest of the anti-crime team. When they made it down, the security guard came over, saying to us that the kids had run out when we went in. He wanted to alert us, but he said he doesn't go into the building. When we asked him about the room on the 3rd floor, he said that's where the old lady's 911 calls come from. We all looked at each other as the color drained from our faces.

It was all too much for me and it activated something inside due to my connection with things spiritually. I found myself obsessed with that building and would drive past it all the time. As I did, I could hear the trapped souls whispering, giggling, playing, and scheming from beyond the brick walls and copper cladding. They wanted me to come back inside. I always kept driving and never went back, even if we were called there for a job. I'm not sure what it did to me, but I also began to be able to hear or see what people were thinking.

It was enough to drive me mad, but I did my best to shut out the noise and use it to our advantage. When out on calls and dealing with some of the violent people on the streets, I began to call them out on their thoughts before they acted. From then on, it was extremely rare that I had to use any force on anyone. Most of them would stand there like a deer in headlights when I'd look them dead in the eyes and say, "Don't even try it."

I could sense the negative energy and thoughts percolating in their minds, all while trying to lower our defenses so that they can assault us. My partner and other cops would look at me as if I were a freak, but I didn't care. It kept us out of trouble 99% of the time. From then on, the only force I had to use was when other cops were already fighting and called for help. While this newfound ability worked well on the job, things were tough at home.

It's not like the movies, and I couldn't see or communicate with dead people. However, I became hypersensitive to the things around me ever since going into the abandoned sanatorium. I could sense more spiritual activity within our house and could even feel them staring at me in my sleep. It put a big strain on the relationship at home also, because just like the criminals on the streets, I was able to sense whenever Jenn or anyone else was being dishonest with me. I couldn't turn it off and had no control over it. It wasn't as if I was being paranoid since it was very accurate, but it became invasive to others. I wished to return to a world where I had limited knowledge. It's easier to be a happy person when you're less aware, but it kept piling on.

A year or so prior to this, I had a kid die in my arms after getting hit by an SUV. There was nothing I could do since the injuries were so severe. All I could do was hold him until the ambulance arrived. The driver wept in his arms off to the side, while we secured the scene and called for the Highway Unit to investigate. As patrol, we didn't investigate or do the paperwork for fatal accidents. It was something that I thought I had put behind me. However, every time we drove past the scene since our haunted "adventure" in the hospital, I could sense him standing there, looking at us as we drove by.

One night while asleep, I was back at the scene of the accident, and he was in my arms. His eyes opened and he turned his head to look at me. "Leave this place," he said with a guttural tone as he struggled to talk. I woke up and immediately started crying. I couldn't take it anymore and didn't want a new ability. I was tired of everything, even from when I was a kid. It was too much, and I wanted it gone. Instead of feeling blessed, I felt cursed, and it had an impact on everyone around me.

I needed help and had to find out some answers, but before doing so, I took the kid's advice to "leave this place," and applied for the Harbor Unit.

Chapter 25: Rough Seas

Jenn and I came onto the job during a very odd time. When we first graduated from the academy and went to our prospective precincts, seniority meant something, and we were at the bottom of the totem pole. As we accrued more time, the senior officers earned their next assignments or retired, while the rookies took our spots at the bottom. Somewhere in between, our classmates were all lost in the shuffle as rookies jumped over us in terms of getting preferential training and assignments. It was an odd place to be, and many of us felt stuck.

The stresses of the job were starting to get to us at home as we started to hit dead ends career-wise. Jenn had put in for ECT (Evidence Collection) while I was applying for Harbor. In typical fashion with the games the NYPD were playing at that time, her application "disappeared", and it went nowhere. The precinct commanders weren't letting cops leave in fear of a "brain drain" experience-wise. We were the last of the few classes to be trained by old-school NYPD cops, and with the older guys gone, we were lost in this void. It didn't matter if you were a hard worker and dependable. Sometimes that made things even worse for you and harder to get out, since they depended on you too much.

I ran into the same problem when it came time to get my application signed off for Harbor. My supervisor wrote this beautiful story about how much of a good cop I was, how active I was arrest-wise, and how I needed little to no supervision. When it came time to check off the recommendation, he checked off "recommended" instead of "highly recommended". To get called for an interview, you needed to be highly recommended. I approached him about it, and he played it off as if he was doing me a favor with the nice story about me. I explained to him that by checking the "recommended" box, I'd never be seen. He responded by saying, "Well I can't lose you, I need you here." He knew exactly what he was doing, and this was the game being played everywhere.

With all this happening, things between Jenn and I started to fall apart. We had been married long enough to the point where it was time to discuss having a family and when to start trying. It had been discussed prior as far as whether we wanted kids, so I wasn't expecting any problems. I wanted a big family, and Jenn was more on the line of "let's take it one at a time and see where it goes". I was fine with that, but when push came to shove, things began to get weird. She began to get cold feet about having kids, and it took a toll on the marriage. With everything going on at work and everything I went through, I was able to sense more than most and knew something was terribly wrong.

"Rough seas" is the best way to describe what was going on at the time. It felt as if I were in a washing machine and getting hit on all sides by large, crashing waves. Life at home was very tense, and the relationship with my partner at work was falling apart as well. The disembodied voices and dreams got even more intense as I tried to fight the Universe, make sense of it all, and hold on too tight to the things I loved most. It all happened at once and I felt like I was sinking. However, in all the chaos, the current was still taking me somewhere.

ROUGH SEAS

One day out on patrol with my partner, their phone rang. They began talking to whomever was on the other end. My partner turned to me and asked, "Could you help my friend? I don't want to deal with this right now." It had to do with a stolen car that became something bigger. To protect those involved, I can't go any further as to what transpired exactly. However, the entire case resulted in me getting into an off-duty incident. It happened on the very day I was driving down to One Police Plaza to drop off my Harbor Unit application. It was a "good" off-duty incident, and I did nothing wrong, but the circumstances behind it had major implications, and it had to be "buried".

I thought nothing else of it and continued my fight to get out of the muck and mire at home and at work. A lot of times, especially when you're just a "grunt" on patrol, there is no recognition, not even an "atta-boy". This was one of those times and life simply went on. I continued to fight with my partner at work and in a "cold war" with Jenn at home. I was stuck in a storm, and the current was bringing me further out into its tentacles.

When I walked into the precinct one day in late spring, I had a message waiting for me to call the chief. This particular chief was very adamant about not getting a certain number of civilian complaints in a specific span of time. I thought the message was for me to call him about a false complaint I got while on vacation. Something had happened one night while I was away, and they forgot to take me off the roll call. To adjust, they put my name on the "change sheet" stating I was on vacation.

The person made a blanket complaint against the entire platoon. Whomever was investigating it, thought that the sergeant was "covering" for me by manually writing me in on vacation. Long story short, I had to show proof that I was in Key West when this all happened, but it stays on your record regardless. I groaned to myself and called the chief, ready to explain the entire nonsense story to him.

"Hey Chief, I'm sorry about all of this. This is what happened," I said to him apologetically while trying to cut him off at the pass. "What are you talking about, kid? I wanted to thank you for what you did a couple of months ago," he replied. "Thank you, sir. Everyone kept dropping the ball, and I knew something was wrong, so I just kept going until someone would help," I said. I thought he might be annoyed that other units looked bad. "No, no, I haven't seen someone from patrol do that and not give up. You did the right thing. We're very proud of you," he said while ensuring I was in the right.

As the conversation felt like it was about to end, he blurted out and asked, "So where do you wanna go? We could use a guy like you in Borough Crime." Borough Crime was like our anti-crime unit in the precinct, except it covered the entire borough. It was a plain-clothes unit which took on all the gang, drug, and gun activity. It was also a path to the detective squad career-wise. Oddly, it was one of the things I told my dad I wanted to do in my career during my conversation with him as a newbie.

I was at a fork in the road. I had gotten into something so big off-duty, I was faced with a choice. Something had happened in the city several months prior that was very controversial, and the political winds blew the wrong way for the cops involved. Seeing what they went through, I could see myself in the same position if I had done work in plain-clothes. Having processed that in my head during the conversation with the chief, I thanked him for the opportunity and turned it down. "Thank you for that, Chief. I don't mean to insult you, but I have my application in for Harbor, and I'd rather wait it out." "Harbor?" he asked in surprise. "Why would you want to go to Harbor? You're so young! You're gonna go there and do nothing for the rest of your career?" the chief added.

ROUGH SEAS

"Well, sir. I've been on boats my entire life and I wouldn't go there to do nothing," I said while fiercely but respectfully defending my stance. "Ok, kid. Come down here and show me your credentials," he said while sighing in a disappointed way. Like the cornerman in the Golden Gloves, the chief said to me before hanging up, "I hope you know what you're doing, kid." The next day I brought down my paperwork and he made a phone call. I was going to Harbor.

Even with me getting into a one-in-a-million incident and receiving the choice assignment of my life, turmoil ruled every day. It was supposed to be a joyous moment, but I still had to deal with the things going on at home and in the precinct. My wife was stuck on patrol while I was going to my "dream" assignment soon. The supervisor at work in the 100th Precinct was incensed that his plan to keep me there failed; then my partner and I broke up. I was in hostile territory all around me and it would be a long 5 months.

In the meantime, I still had to get through the gauntlet of interviewing for Harbor as the chief told me that I had to do everything the right way. He didn't want me to get special treatment and wanted me to earn it like I've earned everything else. When the Housing sergeant heard I was interviewing for Harbor, he took me aside and told me he was there for a short time. He helped me prepare for the interview process and told me what to expect. "They're going to treat you like shit. They'll try to get you all riled up to see how you react," he cautioned. "Just stay calm and get through it. You know your stuff about boats, you'll be fine."

The night before my Harbor interview, the desk sergeant kept me inside to keep me out of trouble. He wanted to make sure I was safe and got there in time for the morning interview. We had a bunch of prisoners in the holding cell, and they asked me to do a prisoner transport with another guy. We brought the guys out in shackles, into the van, and up to central booking in Queens. On the way back we stopped for Chinese food so that I could have a bite to eat while on the desk.

When we exited the car, a cab skidded out while pulling up to the precinct. The driver got out, bleeding from his head, and yelled, "I just got robbed, that's the guy over there, he's got a gun!" In my head I was like "ughghgh" while looking at the cop I was working with. The cop took off like a jackrabbit after the robbery suspect, and there was no way I was catching up to my "track star" partner. I jumped back into the van, caught up, and told the other cop to get in. When we got close enough and the suspect was running out of steam, we leapt out and gave chase on foot.

He was running with the gun in his hand and jumped in front of a car on the freeway. The driver slammed on his brakes and the suspect tried to force himself into the car by banging on the window with his gun. I had my gun out and was ready to take the shot. My service weapon was a Glock 19, and my finger was on the 2nd stage of the trigger when I realized there was a little girl in the back seat. It was dark and the risk was high if I missed or there was a ricochet. I didn't know if I should take the shot or not, but the suspect made the choice for me. He bolted again and ran up the side street. When we closed in on him, he tossed the gun, and we tackled him to the ground. I picked up the gun, and it was an imitation Smith & Wesson pistol.

Had I got into a shooting that night, my career would've essentially been over. There would've been no Harbor interview the next morning and no Harbor assignment in the future. My partner that night took the collar (arrest) so that I could go on my interview. I stuck with him all night to help with the paperwork, before leaving to go into Manhattan. On zero sleep and now on hour 16 of my shift, I sat for the most important interview of my life.

When I got to headquarters, the first thing they asked was, "You look kinda pale, are you alright?" I explained to them that I worked around the clock on a collar my partner and I made. The administrative person laughed and said, "Alright, we'll see if we can get you in first and get you out, so that you can get some sleep." I thanked her and then in typical NYPD form, I sat there all day and was one of the last guys to go. I walked into the room, and they all stared at me as I looked half-dead.

I ran through the panel of questions by the board consisting of sergeants, lieutenants, and the commanding officer. Things seemed to be going well, and they were impressed with my answers, but there was one guy who had to be a dick. I was prepared for it as my Housing sergeant warned me ahead of time. "I see here you work in the 100th Precinct," he said while glancing through my folder. "What could you possibly do over there?" he added snidely. Inside my mind I was saying to myself, "Is this guy fucking kidding me?" but on the outside I said, "Well, my partner and I made a gun collar last night and we closed out a robbery pattern."

His face went pale, and he looked at me with a blank stare. "Woah, woah, woah," a captain cut in. "How do you know you closed out a robbery pattern?" I looked at him with a straight face and said, "I'll let you know soon when there aren't any more robberies." The room burst out with laughter, and they all loved my answer except for the lieutenant. His face got beet red and was mad I embarrassed him. I was going to Harbor, and just like everything else up until now, it was a runaway train. The die was cast and nothing was stopping it.

During late fall of 2007, I was officially notified of my transfer to the Harbor Unit. There was one problem; I was going by myself. Going by yourself was a "death sentence" of sorts as it automatically meant that your new coworkers would be suspicious of you. Typically, you'd be in a class with 10-15 guys, and not even a chief's son would get to go in by himself. It was supposed to be a great moment in my life, but I was met with hostility, especially by that lieutenant. He remembered who I was from the interview, and his first words to me were, "What are you doing here?" since not much time had passed between the interview and that moment.

Problems also persisted at home, and things continued to fall apart with Jenn. My senses and intuition were going off like you wouldn't believe, and I felt betrayed. I wasn't shy about it and called her out on what I thought was going on. Instead of tears and apologies, she handed back my grandma's ring to me. All the things that worked out cosmically to bring us together, were gone. "It's over," I thought to myself. I had everything I ever wanted in life, except a wife and a family of my own.

PART V

Chapter 26: The Guide

Any cop will tell you that when life goes to shit at home, you immerse yourself in the job. The mind goes into "protection-mode" to avoid thinking about the things ripping you into shreds one tiny piece at a time. I was no different and became hyper-focused on proving myself at work to earn my keep in the Harbor Unit. I was already at a disadvantage coming into Harbor by myself because there was a level of mistrust, but there was also a clash of personalities.

Because of how I grew up, where I came from, and being the victim of bullying as a young kid, I refused to play into the hands of those types of people at work. In many cases, the NYPD was like the 13th grade of high school or worse, with all these cliques and childish behavior at times. At a time when I was trying to gain their trust, one of the ringleaders tried to befriend me.

It came at a cost as he said to me one day after seeing me in the hallway with another cop, "Don't talk to that guy, he's no good." The guy he pointed out was a good person, and I never had a problem with him, so my answer to ringleader was, "I'll talk to whomever I want." That wasn't the right answer, and I paid for it almost for the rest of my time there.

On top of that, the chief at the time wanted to create a new "detail" which focused on the south shore of the city. The purpose of it was to try and tamper the issue with reckless jet-skiers, property crimes, and boat accidents. Being new to the unit and having experience along the south shore, I was "volun-told" to do it. A few new guys were given a choice; put in for the detail and we could keep our current squads, or wait to be forced into it, and they would jumble things around. I knew that if I didn't "volunteer" for it, they'd change my squad. I'd wind up with different days off than Jenn, and my marriage would officially be over.

The rules in this new detail were simple, "Take this plastic fishing boat out to post, write 6 summonses a season instead of the normal 4, and keep people from killing themselves." It seemed simple enough, but it created a wedge between us and the other Harbor cops for several reasons. It gave us the freedom they never had, and nobody bothered us if we were doing our jobs. They also had a big problem with the number of summonses we were writing. They felt it made them look bad, even though it was only 2 tickets more per year.

The entire way of thinking was ridiculous and juvenile, but they chose to "die on that hill" and complained about it for years to come. They had forgotten what it was like to be on patrol and had to find things to complain about, especially if it was about someone they didn't like. Regardless, we forged forward, did our job, and to the chief's delight, the number of accidents plummeted. In fact, there was a stretch of years where there were 0 accidents on our post, and property theft was whittled down to hardly anything.

The entire project on the chief's part was a success, so they upgraded us to a 20-year-old 27' Boston Whaler that was initially used for BWI enforcement in the 1980s. It was like having a 1960s muscle car with big engines. The boat rode hard enough to crack your teeth, but it was ours and we loved it. They gave it to us towards the end of the summer in 2008 and we had it for the 2009 season as well. Winter was coming and it started a string of activity at work that was "supernatural" at minimum.

Flight 1549, the "Miracle on the Hudson", was the first of 4 "air disasters" I had been part of over the next 3 1/2 years. While I missed the initial landing on the water and the miraculous events that cold afternoon, my partners and I were tasked with looking for the missing engine. We did so along with the FAA/NTSB and our SCUBA team. It was a long few days as we trolled side-scan sonar devices up and down the Hudson River in the icy cold conditions.

Chunks of ice the size of cars flowed down from underneath the George Washington Bridge, bouncing up against the 36' aluminum boat we were using for this assignment. Most of us wound up getting sick due to exposure, but with good teamwork, we found the missing motor after marking 3 distinct objects matching the motor's dimensions. The first dive SCUBA conducted on object #1 wound up being a submerged car. Thankfully, object #2 was the engine and the guys didn't have to do a 3rd dive in the frigid waters of the Hudson.

After a long winter at work and at home, I was ready to get some sun and warmth on my face as a new summer season arrived. They say, "be careful what you wish for", and I got my wish in the form of our busiest season yet. In July, we had a rare summer nor'easter which held temperatures in the 60s with stiff winds and scattered heavy rain. While we were heading out to post, we saw a sailboat going out into the inlet despite the forecast. I turned to my partner and said, "That's going to be a rescue later." A few hours later we got called for the same sailboat taking on water. The Coast Guard was dispatched too, and although our boat was not made to handle seas that rough, we attempted to make it out.

Things didn't go very well, and we got hit by a large wave abeam (broadside) our first attempt trying to get out of the inlet. It hit us with such force that the wave bent the rail of the rear sliding door. We had no choice but to limp back inside and wait for the Coast Guard to come with their 47' MLB (Motor Lifeboat) to make the rescue. Their boat was designed for weather such as this and could "right" itself if capsized. Before the Coast Guard arrived, another NYPD Harbor boat, a 55ft'er, tried to make it out as well. Those boats are more like river boats and not designed for rough seas. A large wave crashed over the top of their flybridge; prompting them to turn around and wait with us.

The chief at the time was pissed we couldn't make it out, but when he saw the action from above in one of our choppers, he knew we made the right decision. As for us, if we got rolled, we would've been trapped due to the damaged door. It was the right call as we let the Coast Guard do their thing; then we guided the boat to port in calmer waters. We spent the next few hours trying to repair the door so that we could make it back to the base with less of a risk.

During the following month, we avoided a tragedy by having to take part in something gruesome. Every day we would spend our meal at Venice Marina in Brooklyn. We'd tie-off on the docks, eat our food, and fill out the various logs and paperwork required of us. The NYPD loves their paperwork, and we had the "launch" log, memo book, and anything related to boat inspections or tickets we wrote. It was monotonous and redundant, but it was also a nice break to sit at the docks and bullshit with the public.

We had gotten to know the jet ski community over the past year or so and this also helped to tamper down on the reckless behavior. We showed them discretion by giving out warnings before tickets. In return, they respected us by not going too crazy out there. Everything was fine until a fight broke out between the jet skiers at the docks. We were in a big blue boat which said "NYPD" in big letters, but they didn't care. Our meal was interrupted, and we had to fly out of the boat to break up the fight. These were all guys we knew, and we had no idea why they were fighting.

The following day, we were heading out to post near Coney Island, when the call for a plane/helicopter collision came over the air. We immediately turned around and started heading up there in our 27' Boston Whaler. The boat skipped across the water as we maxed out the throttle and RPMs. We were going so fast, only a sliver of the hull and the propellers were touching the water. The engine alarms went off, but it didn't matter. We had to get up there as fast as we could. The only other boats on duty at the time were our slower-moving ones.

We got up there so fast, we wound up being the first boat on scene along with another one a few seconds after. It was too late. The two airframes had sunk to the bottom of the Hudson River off Hoboken, NJ. There was nothing left aside from some floating debris, sneakers, and other things I will not mention. It was a horrible day for the victims and their families. This was the last shift before my vacation, and I was looking forward to a quiet day. Instead, we were faced with tragedy and the "heaviest" job I've had yet since taking the oath.

Any type of air disaster is treated like a crime scene, even if it were an accident. Every piece of debris, clothing, and otherwise, must be collected for the investigation. Over the course of the next few hours, our boat and others did the tedious work of collecting anything afloat, then bringing it back to the west side of Manhattan. It wasn't a selfish moment by any stretch, but I thought to myself, "I can't believe this is the last thing I see before vacation." I knew other people had it worse than I, especially the victims and family, but it was depressing regardless.

During the afternoon on the same day and time we typically did our paperwork at Venice Marina in Brooklyn, the jet skiers got into another argument. This time, one of the guys we knew pulled out a gun and started shooting at everyone. The crazed gunman slowly walked throughout the docks, hunting those who "wronged" him, and even shot at innocent bystanders diving into the water. Knowing what we know, plus what happened the day before, he wouldn't have cared if we were there or not. We would've had no choice but to grab our H&K MP5 submachine guns off the dashboard, and light him up.

Maybe he would've gone after us first as we had our heads buried in paperwork. Taking us out first would've allowed him to go for his intended targets afterwards. Nobody knows what would've happened, but I do know that one tragedy saved us from another. After learning about the shooting, I was able to help identify the suspect who was on the run after killing a man and leaving another in critical condition. We had all the names of those involved in the fight the day prior, and of all the names, he was the only one missing. After contacting the detective squad, they knew who they were looking for, and captured him in another state.

My entire vacation was spent with all of this on my mind. On one side of my brain were the images of the crash, and what we saw when they lifted the mangled wreck out of the water. On the other side, was how something took us away from getting shot or getting into a shooting. We could've easily kept going to our post that day, and nobody would've said anything since we were so far away. It was just another thing on top of everything else that had steered me in a certain direction. I was not in a good mindset after that.

I needed to understand what was going on in the big scheme of things Universe-wise and what was protecting me. Jenn's aunt happened to be friends with a woman who was a spiritual guide, and helped people get their abilities under control. I was a burden to other people and a burden to myself, because I lived with this daily. There were too many things happening and too much "data" coming in. Although Jenn and I were on the rocks, we went to see this woman together so that she could further understand what I was going through.

I didn't know what I was walking into, but we went to the guide's house for our first meeting. When I knocked on the door, she was expecting us. Not because she was a psychic, but because Jenn's aunt arranged the meeting. She had a very calm and soft-spoken demeanor to herself, and welcomed us by saying, "Hi Ben and Jenn, I'm Pat, welcome to my home. Follow me and we'll get started." We walked in, followed her to the left, and into a library-like room with a large group of people in a circle.

She introduced us to the group, and we introduced ourselves back. Pat then asked me what I'd like to get out of the group, so I explained what was going on. My initial goal was to turn off my abilities because I wanted them gone. I didn't want to be helped anymore, and I didn't want to see anything anymore. When I explained it to the group and to Pat, she looked at me with empathy and a sad expression as well. "I'm sorry you're having such a rough time with this, but please don't wish it away. You've been blessed with something and although it's hard for you to handle, we're going to teach you how to get control over it," she said.

I was skeptical, but over the course of the next year, she taught me how to shut out the noise. By shutting out the noise, it allowed me to focus on the day-to-day things going on in this world. Being able to filter through the noise didn't mean I was turning it off; it just allowed me better control over it. Instead of being an invasive thing that ran my life, this force became a supplement to assist me. Over time, the disembodied voices stopped, and the dreams subsided. It began to feel instinctual and more comfortable to me mentally.

The classes also allowed me to foster better relationships with people at work as I settled into my role. Instead of weirding-out my partners who were along for this cosmic ride with me, they felt more comfortable, and we had a great working environment. As I grew happier, more comfortable with my gift, and more in-tune with things going on, I decided to have a talk with Jenn even though I'm not the forgiving type.

Throughout this entire journey and going to the classes, I believe she came to some realizations and became more honest with herself. Jenn was never in a relationship like we had and hadn't lived on her own before meeting me. It was a big change for her, and she was afraid of the next step. Plus, living with someone who has the ability that I do, can't be an easy thing.

We talked about it all and Jenn told me she was afraid to have kids because she thought she wouldn't be a good mother. She felt as if she didn't have the motherly instinct. I knew she was wrong, and I wouldn't have married her if that was the case. Without "reading" her again and successfully fighting the urge to do so, I put my grandma's ring back on her finger, and we moved forward. That winter, we moved together into a new place in Long Beach.

About a week before typing to this chapter in the book, Pat passed away from cancer. I was in shock when Jenn came into the office and told me as I was typing. I know she's still with us and all of those she helped through the years. Pat, I want to thank you for everything you've done for us and others. You saved my life and my marriage. If it weren't for you and all the things going on around me, I wouldn't be where I am today. You taught me how to embrace the blessings given to me, and I surely needed it after the final class I attended.

Chapter 27: A Date With Special Ops

During late spring of 2010, the Harbor Unit upgraded our 27' Boston Whaler after blowing up the motors responding to the aircraft collision in Hoboken. The NYPD received 5 new 31' SAFE Boats with twin 350hp outboards, and we were lucky enough to receive one of them for our detail. With the upgrade came an increase in responsibility since this was a bigger, faster boat and capable of more functions. Initially our detail was coined "Jamaica Bay" since that was our primary responsibility, but now it evolved into "Ocean Response".

Having that boat was like being the pilot of an F-16 multi-role fighter jet. It's speed, handling, and predictability made it seem as if you became part of the machine instead of just getting on a boat and operating it. Launch #315 became our steady SAFE Boat. We also "customized" it more to suit our specific needs. Aside from some equipment upgrades, my partner K-Fed also tinted the windows. When people saw the tinted windows and "L315" across the sides, they knew it was us and knew to behave. If we wanted to or had to, we could chase down almost anything on the water aside from a cigarette boat.

It wasn't all about policing. The boat itself became an attraction, and everyone asked us about it. Just to keep people on their toes, we never divulged the boat's full capabilities, but everyone was happy to see us for the most part. With a new mission and more professional look, it became oddly like how we were treated when doing Critical Response in Manhattan. People would wave us over to their docks to talk and offer us water or food. We made a lot of friends down there, especially at Gateway Marina in Brooklyn.

After getting a call for service and helping one of the tow companies bring back a disabled boat, a woman with blonde hair waved us down to come over. She was with a motley group of people all hanging around their boats, grilling food, and telling fish stories. Her name was Jennifer, and it turned out that she was a cop in the NYPD Special Operations Division. Special Ops was the "mothership" for all the specialized units which included Aviation, Mounted, ESU, K9, and us in Harbor.

We would swing by when there was some down-time if we saw Jennifer and her friends out there. One guy there was a Cuban immigrant, and we started talking about Key West somehow. It turned out that he loved the place just as much as I did. We'd sit there during our break and talk about the island all the time. We knew the same restaurants, people, and fishing spots. Jennifer interrupted us one day to show us a funny trick with a giant white goose at the dock. She had named it "Arturo", and when she called out "Arturo!" at the top of her lungs, he would waddle down the docks to hang out with us.

Jennifer and I had some good laughs until one day I thought I had pissed her off. She broke out into a story about Far Rockaway, and I started laughing and making fun of her. Her demeanor changed and with a serious face, she barked, "Hey! You can't make fun of Rockaway!" I responded as fast as I could, "Sure I can, I'm from there!" "No you're not," she replied. "Yes I am. I was born there, my dad grew up there, and my grandma lived there until she moved to Florida," I said. She snapped back, "Who's your grandma?" I replied while pointing to my name patch, "Harriet Reiver."

Her eyes grew big, and her jaw dropped. "Harriet?!" she said with astonishment. "Your grandma and my Aunt Mimi were best friends! They moved down to Florida together and wound up living in the same building!" she exclaimed. I started thinking in my head and realized Mimi was my grandma's friend on the next floor below. I was at her place all the time when I went down to Florida. We used to alternate having dinner in their apartments. It was incredible to me that all this time, our families had known each other for almost 90 years.

We became good friends after figuring out the connection. I told her about *my* Jenn and how she was stuck in the 107th Precinct. We began to brainstorm, thinking of ways to get her out of there. The precincts were still playing games with applications and transfers. There was no way out unless you knew somebody or got into something big. Jenn was still suffering from health problems with her hands and alternating time between patrol/desk duty. The chances of her getting into anything big were slim to none.

Jennifer, knowing the story of how I got into Harbor, joked around that maybe if I got into something big again, I could ask to get my Jenn off patrol. We wound up having a very busy summer and made countless rescues, but there was nothing high-profile that would rise to the occasion of another favor. It was hopeless. While Jenn and I were patching things up and our relationship started to improve at our new home, she still felt trapped at work while I enjoyed what I was doing.

September rolled around and the season was wrapping up. We were in autumn-mode as we geared up for presidential visits and the U.N. General Assembly. On the first day of autumn on September 22, 2010, the President was making his rounds across New York City. We had our typical assignment for the event, which was to secure the bridges of any hypothetical route the President may take in a motorcade emergency. Every aspect of NYPD Special Ops was utilized to protect the President and dignitaries during the U.N. meetings.

During the afternoon while we were at the Gerritsen Creek bridge near Gateway Marina, one of our choppers was coming in to refuel. The quiet, warm day, consisting of me relaxing with a cigar and a sub-machine gun, was quickly interrupted. "10-13! 10-13! We have a chopper down by Floyd Bennett Field!" the radio blared. I threw my cigar into the water, put the gun on the dash, and took the helm. I turned to my partner and said, "Pull out all of the PFDs (life vests) from underneath and get them ready." I hit the throttle and raced to help our brothers and sisters in the chopper.

Having worked the horrors of the helicopter collision a year prior, I had no idea what to expect. My hands gripped the wheel so tight, that my knuckles were turning white and purple. The throttle was pinned, and the trim was set as high as it could go without the propellers cavitating. Thankfully these were new motors and a new boat, so no engine alarms went off as we hit 60+ mph around the Marine Parkway Bridge. When we made the turn to head up to Floyd Bennett Field, we saw a busted-up NYPD chopper with its floats activated.

Luckily it didn't capsize, and the floats inflated simultaneously. This is a common problem, and we've seen it happen in other incidents. We got up there within a minute or two and began to assist a small fishing boat that came over to help. One of the main rotor blades snapped in half and the front windshield was caved in. My partner, K-fed, always missed the big stuff, and my other partner was in that day. He did a great job getting the rest of the crew members out, including the pilot, as I maneuvered the boat to get as close as possible. It was a delicate operation as I had to make sure we didn't puncture the floats and/or get taken down by a potentially sinking helicopter.

Once we had the remaining chopper crew on L#315, we pulled away from the empty chopper and dropped them off at the boat ramp. The small fishing boat did the same and we thanked them for assisting us. It turned out that when the chopper was coming in for fuel, a gear in the transmission cracked and the main rotor seized up. As the chopper was falling out of the sky, the pilot manually engaged the floatation devices. Her decision probably saved lives and all we had to do was get everyone safely off the chopper.

The stage was set and although we didn't want any recognition, it was just enough to put our names in the spotlight. My partner that day wanted to go to the Harbor "Adam" base in Howard Beach, which gave him a better commute. He got his wish and went there after the season fully wrapped up. As for me, I asked for help getting Jenn off patrol. It was the opening we needed for my friend Jennifer to help us out. She was able to get me a meeting with the Special Ops lieutenant.

There happened to be a spot open on the midnight shift at Special Ops, which meant that Jenn and I wouldn't work the same shifts anymore. I was assured that it was only to get her foot in the door. I was also told that she would have to go through the process like everyone else and fill out an application. I gave her the news, and she filled out the application right away. Just as with her application to ECT, her precinct tried to play games again, and paperwork went missing.

Thankfully I had the right people on my side, and a phone call was made. The very next day, one of Jenn's supervisors was waiting at the desk, all-while saying in a kiss-ass tone, "Here Jenn, I have everything for you!" They weren't playing any games at Special Ops, especially with *this* chief in charge. The paperwork was handed in, and 8 months later during May of 2011, Jenn was finally off patrol.

The precinct took it personally and they never called to notify her of the transfer. I got a call from one of the Special Ops sergeants looking for her. Luckily, I was in the good graces of the "mothership", and they extended her the same courtesy. Jenn arrived and never looked back. It was the assignment she needed. In more ways than one, it was the assignment we *both* needed.

Chapter 28: Harbor Charlie

During the winter of 2010 into 2011, my partners and I spent a leisurely time around Manhattan trying to stay warm. Whenever you told another cop that you were in Harbor, the standard reply was, "Oh, must be nice." It was nice, when it wasn't wintertime. Winters around the waters of New York City were brutal. Biting wind, frigid water, and cold metal boats, would combine to make for a very chilly environment. Staying dry was essential, because if you got your socks or pants wet, there was no drying off, and you'd be miserable for the rest of the day.

The Ocean Response detail would shut down due to the lack of boating activity along the south shore. They would farm us out around the city to cover the gap which occurred during the change of shifts. We would also cover the counter-terrorism operations and hang out at spots considered soft targets. One of those locations was North Cove Marina by "Ground Zero" in lower Manhattan. It was one of my favorite spots to be during the winter as we could walk up to the atrium and get some hot food or coffee.

Another nice feature for the season, was the yacht we would dock next to during the entire winter. It was a beautiful old yacht that could cross the Atlantic without refueling. Over time, the crew befriended us, and we used to hang out with them all the time.

Most of them were British and Australian, and they were just as curious about us as we were about them. They'd tell us stories about life on the yacht and how they got into the business. In the same respect, we answered questions about what it was like to work on the NYPD boats. The hot tea and conversation kept us warm as we spent our mealtime in opulent luxury and fine company. It was the perfect distraction from the stresses at home.

Jenn was unaware she'd get transferred to Special Ops in May, so she was "chomping at the bit" to get off patrol. She was looking forward to being off the streets, getting better rest, and the prospect of her hands healing a little bit. We had also decided that now was the time to start trying for a family. When she went to the doctor to get a full physical and the "ok" to start trying, her bloodwork came back with a problem, and we were told to wait. Thyroid issues were common with her autoimmune disease, and her levels were dangerously off. We were told that if we started trying for a kid now, Jenn would either lose the baby, or the baby could be born with severe deformities. The news was rough, but we had waited so long, we were willing to wait longer if need be.

Once Jenn started Special Ops in May, it was a hectic time for all the units attached to the mothership. Even though she was on midnights at the time, she got a firsthand look at the largest operation of late spring, Fleet Week. It was a big deal for everyone involved as we were all tasked with securing the Navy ships, guiding them in safely, and standing guard for the following week. The event always happened on or around my birthday. I was never off, and vacation picks didn't exist due to my lack of seniority.

I would spend my 35th birthday on the boats, then in the hospital due to a sudden and severe illness. During that time, I was trying to take off any winter weight gained by staying sedentary on the boats, all while feasting with the yacht crew. It was then that I learned that eating salad was more dangerous than bacon. During the first week of June while Jenn was doing her midnight shifts, I developed severe abdominal pain and a high fever after eating some leafy greens. At first, I thought it was a summer flu, but the fever never broke. I tried to go to work and sleep it off in the boat cabin, but things just kept getting worse.

About 3 days into it, the pain started to wrap around my back, and up to my chest. I called Jenn at work and told her that I was taking myself to the hospital. When I arrived, they initially thought I had appendicitis, so they immediately began pumping me full of antibiotics while prepping me for a CT scan. The scan revealed that I had inflammation throughout my intestines, but the appendix was ok. Overall, I spent the next week in the hospital with a 104 degree fever as they tried to figure out what was wrong.

All the tests were coming back negative, and they contributed it to the antibiotics in my body for a couple of days before doing the cultures. This was not a good hospital, and stories like mine were common. I wound up having a fever for a total of 9 days between home/work and the hospital before it finally broke. They believe the illness was caused by E. Coli. Had I not taken myself to the hospital, they said I would've wound up with sepsis and gone into cardiac arrest. It sounded serious, but as soon as I was without a fever for 24hrs, they told me to see my own doctor and kicked me out. When Jenn came to get me from the hospital, I was sitting alone on the curb with a "Get Well" balloon.

Regardless of whether I was home or not, I felt horrible physically and it took me a while to recover. I could hardly eat anything and every time I did, I would get abdominal pain as my body digested food. On top of it all, the job never had me in their books as "hospitalized" despite the fact that the NYPD district surgeon had come to visit me in the hospital. When you're admitted into the hospital, it didn't count as sick time in the NYPD. Because of this administrative error and another earlier that year, it caused me to be labeled as "chronic sick". In the big scheme of things, I knew it was a mistake and would eventually get fixed, but the supervisors in Harbor gave me a hard time about it.

It was a rough patch in my time with Harbor since I was physically ill and unable to perform as expected. The NYPD is notorious for cops going from "hero to zero" in the blink of an eye. With being a "squeaky wheel" because I felt like garbage, combined with being categorized as chronic sick until they straightened it out, I was *that* guy. It felt as if all the good work I did there over the past 3+ years was erased in an instant due to a batch of evil salad.

However, it wasn't all doom and gloom. Jenn and I had an anniversary trip coming up in early July, and we were excited to spend it out in Oregon wine country. I didn't know how I was going to eat or drink, but I was happy to get away and celebrate the first normal year we had together couple-wise in a while. I may have been sick, but she had her dream assignment, and I was in Harbor. It was the perfect moment to get away, take it all in, and be thankful for what we had.

The flight from JFK to Portland, Oregon was early in the morning, and I could hardly look at food. However, Jenn was hungry, so we got a bite to eat at the airport before our flight. Sitting directly next to us was Anthony Bourdain, celebrity chef and known for his travel shows. He was as grumpy as I was, and we were respectful not to bother him as he sipped on his coffee. It was a good omen to me since I was still feeling down, and here sits my favorite TV personality. We got up after eating breakfast and I made eye contact with him. I nodded to him respectfully and he nodded back, then Jenn and I walked to the gate silently starstruck.

We wound up staying in a beautiful bed & breakfast in the heart of the Willamette Valley, and it couldn't be more perfect.

HARBOR CHARLIE

Upon arrival, the host and owner of the house handed us giant glasses of pinot noir. I couldn't resist and we took our glasses to the back porch. The landscape was otherworldly to me, with a lush forest behind us and songbirds everywhere. Rolling hills and gentle mountains ruled the sights, and nighttime was like nothing I've ever seen. I've been to upstate New York and other places, but the sky was so dark and the stars so many, you couldn't make out the constellations.

The trip was perfection, but I could hardly eat. Small bites and small meals would be about as best as I could do without being doubled over in abdominal pain as everything was still healing. It was very deflating, especially being in this "foodie" region and everyone watching me pick at my food. I also had a lot on my mind with work even though I shouldn't have. Around the time I became ill, we got a new chief at Special Ops. Being out of work for several weeks, going on vacation, and being designated "chronic sick", was not a good way to make a first impression. In my mind, when I returned to work, I'd be "in the weeds" immediately.

I was also tired of explaining to strangers as to why I'm just picking at my food. Thankfully, I only had to tell the story one more time and then people got the message. Jenn and I loved staying at bed & breakfasts when given the chance, but I always found the breakfast part awkward. Sitting at a dining room full of strangers felt like an interrogation room amongst the guests. I'm not a morning person, and I don't particularly like explaining what I do for a living repeatedly.

Things especially get weird when you tell someone that you're an NYPD cop. You become the focus of attention, and they ask you all the typical NYPD TV show questions. One person even asked me if I thought Tom Selleck was a good police commissioner. My eyes rolled back so far into my head, I'm sure the guests saw it. Luckily the breakfast plates were being collected, and it helped interrupt the scene.

"Is there something wrong with the food?" the owner of the bed & breakfast asked me one morning. I groaned on the inside and got myself ready to tell the story again. I was sick and tired of it, so I kept the story short about the food part. However, he was a good interrogator. He hovered over me and wouldn't leave until he got more information. To make him go away, I told him about my apprehensions with work, and what was waiting for me when I got back.

He stepped back from me and did a motion with his hands as if to "poo-poo" my concerns. "Oh nonsense!" he exclaimed. "You're gonna do great. You're gonna get back there and you're gonna do all these great things," as he rattled off a list of personal accomplishments to make the new chief happy; "reclaiming" my spot at the top. He knew nothing about me or the job, so it was odd to me. I was trying to be kind, so I gestured a simple "thank you," as I looked down at my half-eaten food. It was as if something took over his body, especially since he was quiet and gracious up until that point.

We still had a few days of vacation left, and I did my best to relax to enjoy the rest of it. The vineyards we went to helped with that, most notably at Domaine Drouhin. Sipping on their world-class pinot noirs, while staring out at the vineyard and wildflower-lined paths, was a priceless experience. Maybe it was the gallons of wine I consumed, or maybe it was my own personal cheerleader at the bed & breakfast. All I know is that I didn't have a care in the world at that moment. It was "heaven on earth" since it felt as if I were transported to a Tuscan villa in Italy.

We returned to New York, and I was back to work the very next day on July 25, 2011. Another rare nor'easter was impacting the region, but this one was minor compared to the one during July of 2009. It was a very nasty day, and we spent half of the shift running up to the Bronx to get Launch #315 from repair. For the second half, we tied up in the back bay to avoid the steady easterly winds, stinging rain, and 60 degree temperatures. Thankfully we had the SAFE boat and able to crank up the heat, while enjoying some Manhattan clam chowder from one of the local seafood spots.

Towards the end of our shift, Harbor Adam raised us up on the radio to tell us they were having mechanical problems. A thru-hull piece that connects to the rudder, had a leak due to a bad seal, and they were taking on water. They asked us to escort them to the Verrazano Bridge, then hand them off to the Harbor Charlie's patrol boat. Harbor Charlie would then escort Adam up to the shop in the Bronx. Harbor Charlie was the base we left from every day before going out to our Ocean Response post.

"Let's do this escort and bring the boat back to the base after we hand it off to Launch 9," I said to my partner. The weather was so bad, he agreed, and we geared up for a long ride back in the rain and wind; slowly following Harbor Adam towards the Verrazano Bridge. We had to take it "wide" and not run the beach like we normally would on our westward trek. The waves were too nasty as they built up with the help of steady onshore winds. As we were following the other boat, I noticed a strange object in the water about 500-800ft away to our southwest.

"What is that?" I asked my partner. He shrugged his shoulders and replied, "I don't know, wanna check it out?" The water does strange things and can cause optical illusions when objects are on it. From far away, it looked like a piece of debris floating on the water. It could be best described as a floating metal triangle from our vantage point. "Launch 315 to Harbor Adam," I chirped on the radio. "Harbor Adam," they replied. "How are you guys doing over there?" I asked. "We're okay, we have it under control. The leak is slowing down," they replied. "I see something off to our southwest, do you mind if we go check it out?" I asked cautiously. "Sure, what is it?" they replied. "I don't know," I said as we broke off to check it out.

Harbor Adam got further away down the beach as we slowly made our way out into the ocean and into more weather. The object got closer, then started to change visually before revealing itself. "It's a dog!" I yelled to my partner. "It's a dog! Get the dog noose!" I yelled again. My partner exited out of the cabin and got the dog noose ready to attempt a rescue. What looked like a metal triangle hundreds of feet away, wound up being the snout of a dog sticking up out of the rough ocean waters. It was barely keeping afloat and taking its last breaths before sinking to the bottom.

I got the starboard side of the boat right to the dog. My partner got the noose around it, but the wind against the tide began to pull the dog under our boat. "Break it off!" I yelled to my partner as to let the dog go. I pounded the steering wheel in frustration, hoping the dog didn't go under. My partner, soaking wet, looked at me with dejection on his face. "We'll come about and try again!" I yelled out the door.

I swung the ass of the boat around as quickly as I could, hoping to see the dog still there. He was and we gave it another try. My gut feeling was that this was it. If we weren't successful on the second try, the dog was going under due to exhaustion. I crept the boat up about a foot away, but this time I left the boat in gear to match the current and fight the wind. We had seconds to do this, so I leapt out of the cabin while the boat was still in gear. It was an unorthodox and dangerous move, but my partner needed help since it was a big dog. If we missed, the dog was going to be chopped meat courtesy of the spinning props.

My partner got the dog noose back on him, and I put my arms around the dog's body to help pull him in. It was a gorgeous

German shepherd, and I couldn't believe this was happening. We brought the dog into the heated cabin, and we just stood there for a minute in shock. "Launch 315 to Central?" I went over the air. "Launch 315, go," they chirped back. "Show us with a dog? In the middle of the ocean?" I replied in a dumbfounded manner. "Dog in the ocean, 10-4," the dispatcher replied. The radio went nuts as we were getting peppered with questions and supervisors wanted more info.

We didn't have any info, and had no idea where it came from as confusion set in. "Only you," my partner said while soaked, out of breath, and referring to me as always being in the middle of everything. "Let's run the shore along Coney and Brighton. Maybe someone will flag us down," my bewildered partner suggested. "Good idea," I replied. We slowly made our way to the shore while getting lifted and dropped in the big swells.

Meanwhile, the dog was exhausted and leaning up against my leg. You could tell that this shepherd was a guard dog and an expensive one at that. It had a beautiful coat and muscles which were an indicator of the intense training of a work dog. "Please don't bite me, please don't bite me," I whispered to myself. I was in fear that the stressed-out dog would snap and maul us in the cabin with nowhere to go. Imagine rescuing an animal such as this, then having to shoot it if it attacked you. This was one of the millions of things going through my mind, all-while remembering the words of the bed & breakfast owner in Oregon just 2 days prior.

When we neared the beach, we were waved down by someone standing on a jetty. We got as close as we could so that we could hear what they were yelling. It was a friend of the dog's owner, so my partner instructed him to meet us at the docks of Kingsborough College inside of Sheepshead Bay. I took the boat around the corner, and my partner helped me dock it. The dog had no energy and didn't want to get off the boat, so I picked him up and we brought it onto dry land.

The owner and the dog's family came down and thanked us profusely, giving us hugs and kisses. It turned out that they had just picked up the dog from JFK airport via eastern Europe. The dog's name was "Charlie", and it was a 2yr old guard dog that had just completed its training. When they got home from the airport, they opened the door to the SUV, and the dog bolted. They gave chase down to the beach, and when they thought they had Charlie cornered, he went into the ocean instead. The storm and the current dragged him 2 miles out into the ocean from where he originally went in. Oddly, there was no 911 call, and nobody knew what had happened.

As this scene was playing out and we heard that Charlie was in the water for 40 minutes before stumbling upon him, my dad's words, "You might not save the world, but you might save *someone's* world," kept replaying in my head. The timing and circumstances of the rescue were very odd to say the least. The strangest thing of all to me, was how we worked out of Harbor Charlie and the dog's name was also Charlie. It's not a very common name for a guard dog, and I still get chills thinking about the entire incident.

My partner and I wound up being "celebrities" for a short while, and our name was in almost every newspaper around the Country. We wound up on Good Day New York to tell our tale in the TV studio. I remember having to be there in dress uniform at an ungodly hour in the morning to get prepped for our time on camera. Everybody wanted to interview us, and we got tired telling the story, but it was a feel-good moment that the NYPD loved, so we went along with it.

The new chief of Special Ops also took notice, and we received a lot of praise from him. It worked out well for Jenn as I was back

HARBOR CHARLIE

in the spotlight for positive reasons. All the drama of me being out sick the month prior, disappeared in an instant. Even in a positive moment, though, there was pushback from the clique in Harbor. They didn't like the attention we were getting, and they believed it was my fault for finding the dog.

A storm was coming, and in more ways than one.

Chapter 29: Hurricane Irene

The weeks following our "big" rescue of Charlie the German Shepherd, were relatively quiet aside from the leftover fanfare post-rescue. My partners and I continued to do our thing down in Jamaica Bay and out in the ocean if needed. Jenn was happier and healthier as she settled into her new "home" at Special Ops. Also as promised, she was taken off her midnight shifts and put onto days. This allowed us more time together, and it was easier for her to make doctor appointments for bloodwork.

The new chief was very happy with our work, and we continued to be left alone on post compared to the other boats. This, along with the rescue of Charlie, remained a sore spot for some of the other Harbor guys, and the grumbling continued. It didn't help either when we made a BWI arrest in mid-August, and needed everyone's help logistically to complete the task. Making an arrest in Harbor wasn't easy and a logistical nightmare, but we had no choice.

Heading into Sheepshead Bay one day, a fishing boat slammed into a moored and occupied sailboat right in front of us. The guy in the sailboat popped out and yelled, "This guy just hit me and there are beer cans everywhere!" We looked onto the deck of the fishing boat, and over a dozen empty cans, probably way more, were rolling around the deck. My partner for the day took the arrest, while I awaited around for another cop to help me bring the boat up to the Bronx to be impounded.

"You guys are assholes," one of the cops said to me when I got back to the base. "We don't make arrests here," he added. I went over and showed him the arrest log, containing dozens of arrests which Harbor cops had made throughout the years. At this point it was personal, and they didn't care about the circumstances or who did what before us. I had no control over where we were when things happened.

However, I knew that the number of things going on over the past couple of years was unnatural, and it made them feel uncomfortable. For me, it was something that I grew used to and began to accept it with the help of my mentor, Pat. Unfortunately, it didn't matter. You could feel the negativity, and it was very hard to go to work daily. I even went to my dad's old captain, Bernie Weber, for some advice. He was my dad's commanding officer in the 101st Precinct during the 1980s. Bernie had remained a good friend of the family long after his retirement. He always had this Solomon-like wisdom. I believed he could guide me better than my dad, since my dad might avoid the hard truth from me.

I told Bernie what was going on and he shook his head as if to understand. "Do you know your dad went through the same thing?" he told me. "No, I had no idea," I replied. "This is part of the reason why your dad didn't want you to become a cop. He was afraid you'd be just like him and face the same problems. Your dad was a hard worker and took pride in what he did, just like you do now. That's a problem if you work with the wrong people," he said slowly while adding, "You can be the nicest guy in the world, it doesn't matter. There will always be people who don't like you."

"I don't get it," I said while shaking my head. "It's not yours to get," he replied and kept going, "You must do what's right for you regardless of what they think. At the end of the day, you need to be able to retire, look at yourself in the mirror, and say you did it the right way. The rest is all nonsense, I guarantee you." I looked at him and nodded my head. "They can call you every name in the book, but even *they* can't say you were a bad cop or corrupt if somebody asked them. That's the most important thing when it comes to dealing with *them*," he said before giving me a hug and shaking hands. "Thank you, Bernie," I said. "I got ya, kid. Don't you worry, just get through the storm." By storm, he meant figuratively, not literally; at least that's what I thought.

A few days later, a tropical wave formed in the Atlantic. It strengthened quickly off the Lesser Antilles while moving off to the west/northwest. Within a couple of days, it was named Tropical Storm Irene as it neared Puerto Rico. A brushing landfall was made, and the mountainous topography failed to weaken Irene as it quickly became a hurricane. With the help of a cold front to the west and steering mechanisms "just right", it missed another opportunity to weaken near the Dominican Republic. At this point, it began barreling towards the Bahamas as a Category 3 hurricane.

On August 24, 2011, Hurricane Irene wound up jogging west of the Turks & Caicos. It rowed through the lower Bahamas, before heading back out into open water. It was at this point we knew we might have a problem on our hands in the New York City area. Preparations began at all Harbor Unit bases that day and everyone was utilized. My partners and I were taken off our regular post. We were assigned to the base to help them move assets away from Irene's potential path. We were also tasked with securing anything that was left behind for post-storm response.

Irene was still on the move, with the center of the storm going just east of the upper Bahamas. Then it took a more northerly turn towards North Carolina at a higher rate of speed. I closely watched the storm unfold over the next couple of days, and reality had set in. It was time for Jenn and I to prepare. We lived about 2 blocks from the ocean, and the Long Island/New York City area had a history of not handling hurricanes very well. Even "Category 1" hurricanes over the past 100+ years, brought devastation to the region. We had to take it very seriously in case it took a certain path.

I evacuated Jenn and our dog, Marble the Shih Tzu, to her parent's house in East Meadow. Preparations were made at home by unplugging anything electronic, making sure the sump pumps worked, and bringing anything of value up to the second floor. We didn't know what to expect since this was the first storm we had to endure while living in Long Beach. In the area we lived, there was also the potential for the bay to meet the ocean near our house.

It was hard to coordinate everything with Jenn's work shift. Plus, she was on the same alert-status we were on. NYPD Special Ops was waterfront property and on Jamaica Bay, so they weren't sure what to expect flooding-wise. I prepared the house each day before and after my shift. Jenn would commute from East Meadow, before going directly back to her parents to take care of the dog. By the time everything was prepared, Irene had slammed into the Outer Banks of North Carolina, heading our way very rapidly. There was nothing more I could do. I closed the door behind me, locked it, and evacuated to East Meadow as well.

On Saturday August 27, 2011, I was doing a modified shift due to my assignment that day. Jenn was very nervous about the storm. Throughout the years, she had gotten calls from my partner that I've been hurt. Jenn would also get calls from me that I got into something big and would be late. With everything that had happened during my career, she didn't want me out there in the storm. Instead of going up to Croton-on-Hudson, NY to be with my partners, or volunteering to be "Storm Response", I listened to her and took myself out of the game.

HURRICANE IRENE

I volunteered to stay at Harbor Charlie base, adjust lines on the remaining boats, and deal with any storm-surge flooding if need be. If it got too much, we had a plan to evacuate to the Brooklyn Army Terminal, so I was safe regardless. Before heading into work, Jenn and I got to see each other. She hugged me and said, "I love you, Ben. Don't do anything stupid." It didn't matter that I was hanging back at the base, she had to say it anyway. I gave her a kiss, patted Marble's head, and walked out.

On the way in, I listened to the news and the bulletins regarding the hurricane and tropical storm warnings posted. Internally, I was upset that I wasn't upstate with my partners, or at-the-ready for any hypothetical rescue mission. It was the first time I had ever listened to Jenn about something like that. In one aspect, I was doing the right thing by my wife; in another, I felt out of place being on the desk at work. The supervisors knew it too, and they knew it wasn't like me to request an assignment like that.

I walked in, got into uniform, and did some final storm prep at the base. Afterwards, I was post-changed to desk duty. Every cop that walked by, including the ones who didn't like me, all said the same thing. "Are you ok?" they'd ask while thinking I was still sick from the month prior. "I'm fine," I replied, growing angrier with each duplicate question and answer. I must've rearranged the paperwork and radio a half-dozen times, paced around the desk, and doodled avant-garde art on my scrap paper as boredom took over. I felt useless and would feel even worse in several hours.

Every so often, I'd get off the desk, walk to the back door, and stare at the remaining boats during the first flood tide. While it was nothing of concern at that point, it was still high enough where one of the SCUBA guys was able to climb onto the top of the dock pilings. There was still about 3-4 feet of wiggle-room left, but if the water went above that mark, our docks could get destroyed. Winds also began to increase as they swirled around the Brooklyn

Army Terminal and buffeted up against the remaining 4 boats. You could hear the tension in the dock lines as they stretched and creaked with each wind gust.

We were also keeping a close eye on Hurricane Irene itself. She had dipped into North Carolina just enough to weaken it, and the center of the storm was sitting near the Delmarva Peninsula. When hurricanes make landfall, the wind field expands rapidly, and sustained tropical storm force winds were knocking on our door. Like spokes of a bicycle wheel, fast-moving heavy squalls began to make their way into the area. Winds would pick up, heavy rain would fall for a minute or two, then things would calm down before repeating itself again. This pattern was about to end as the main bands from Hurricane Irene, were approaching Sandy Hook, NJ and the Rockaway Peninsula.

I went back to the desk, sat down, and watched TV. The mayor was giving one of his updates to the press as far as storm prep, precautions, and the progress of Hurricane Irene's track. He reiterated that everyone in low-lying areas should evacuate and take the storm seriously. However, there will always be those who ignore the warnings either out of stubbornness, or to test man's strength over nature. We were about to get a taste of the foolishness.

At approximately 7:15pm on August 27th, and as heavy rain bands from Hurricane Irene were approaching the NYC/NJ coast, a 10-54 water rescue came over the air by Mayberry Promenade in Staten Island. A witness had called 911 after seeing two kayakers go out into the storm and disappear into the darkness of Raritan Bay. At this point, the heavy squalls had already taken over the body of water which separates New Jersey and Staten Island. As I sat on the desk and gave out information, crews rushed down to Launch #311 and #351 to respond.

HURRICANE IRENE

There I sat, useless and with no testicles, as these guys went out to brave the storm. As information came in, I continued to give it out as best as I could. However, the two victims couldn't be seen anymore, and we didn't know where they were or what they looked like. A few minutes had passed when the pilot of SAFE Boat #311 went over the air and said that they were returning due to a lost engine. There was nothing heard from the other crew as Launch #311 limped back to the docks with only one engine working.

The phone rang at the desk, and it was hard to hear what they were saying due to the poor signal, wind, and overall background noise. "Ben! We're coming back in and need help tying off the boat. We lost an engine!" the pilot, Billy, yelled so that I could hear him. "Coming right down," I replied. I got off the desk, ran down to the docks, and waited for what felt like an eternity. You could hear the wind overhead whooshing and howling as it failed to reach the surface. Launch #311 finally made the turn into the base and had problems maneuvering due to the lack of a second engine.

Billy did a great job getting the disabled boat to me while his partner, Brian, caught the line I threw to him. We got the bow cleat tied off, and Billy was slowly walking the stern back to me so that we could secure it. There was still nothing from Launch #351 on the radio, and we were getting concerned. I threw the line onto the last cleat, and the engine roared back to life. "The engine started!" Billy yelled as we stood there stunned for a second. "C'mon, c'mon! Get on the boat, we need another guy!" he yelled while motioning with his hands for me to get onboard.

I hopped on and called the sergeant to let them know what was going on. "Go, go!" the sergeant said with urgency in their voice. Billy looked at us and said, "Ok, let's give it another try." We untied the boat, backed away from the docks using extra power due to the wind, and raced around the sea wall of the base. Billy happened to be one of the guys who didn't like me. It was a blend of sweet and sour as he was happy that I helped them dock, but also mad it was me. Regardless, we made our way over to the search area.

It was an eerie feeling to me, and I had a pit in my stomach. I wasn't supposed to be out on the boat since I had taken myself out of the game. My steady partners were also not with me, and I was not with my usual crew. Something was going on like it had in the past and I could feel it. Was I being brought here to this moment to die a "heroic" death? It certainly felt like it as we rode off into the unknown after promising Jenn that I wouldn't do anything stupid.

Heading down towards the Verrazano Bridge wasn't too bad. You could see lightning off in the distance as you looked south, but the water was calmer than I thought it would be. The landmasses of Brooklyn and Staten Island were helping to keep the water to a fine chop, but the wind was buffeting the sides of Launch #311. It was an interesting boat for the supervisors to choose as one of the assets left behind. Its bow rails had been previously removed for repair. If there was a rescue to be made, it would be difficult without anything on the bow to grab onto.

There was still no word from Launch #351 as we were about to cross under the threshold of the Verrazano Bridge, and into the open water. There is an odd phenomenon when crossing under the bridge at night. Visibility is good north of the bridge due to the city lights, but once you cross underneath, the lights dim, and things go black. We crossed the threshold, and things went black due to the storm clouds. Launch #311 was immediately hit with fierce winds, large/confused waves, and heavy rain. There was no choice but to slow down to a crawl as waves and wind battered us.

Being out in the open, there was nothing to protect us anymore. Winds were racing in from the east/southeast "perfectly" in between Sandy Hook and Rockaway. Tremendous swells also heaved up and into the lower harbor. We didn't know where Launch #351 was, but it didn't matter at that point. We were in our own fight as we tried to get to the search area. 20 minutes had already passed from the time I got onto the boat. It should've taken us about 5 minutes to get to where we were; that's how poor the conditions were.

As we were battered by the waves and using our instruments to navigate since we could hardly see, my phone rang in the middle of the chaos. "Ben, turn around, it's too rough," the voice said. Now I could understand why Billy was yelling at me when he called the desk after losing power in the engine. "What?" I asked due to all the background noise. "Ben, you have to turn around, it's too dangerous. I'm ordering you to turn around!" It was a supervisor some of us called "Big Pants", who was on Launch #351.

Concerned about their safety, the first thing I asked was, "Where are you?" He replied, "We're back at the base, you have to turn around." Billy looked at me as we continued to get battered by waves and I said to him, "He wants us to turn around." With a surprised look on his face, Billy yelled, "What?!" "He wants us to turn around," I replied. "We can't turn around. We could get turned over," Billy said to me. I got back on the phone and repeated Billy's concerns to Big Pants. "Sir, it's too dangerous for us to try and turn around where we are!" I yelled over the sound of the rain, wind, and thunder.

I couldn't believe that we were left out there alone. Nobody informed us that the other boat had turned around. "Ben, I'm ordering you to turn around!" he barked again at me over the intense background noise. "We can't sir, it's too dangerous, we have to keep going and find safety somewhere else," I replied. There was a pause on the phone, and I thought I had lost the call in the storm. "Hello?" I said into my phone. "Well, just go out there and make it look like you tried, but if you fuck this up, it's on you!" he exclaimed before hanging up on me.

"What did he say? What did he say?" Billy asked, turning his head to look at me. "He said to give it a try, but if we fuck it up it's on us," I said back to him. "Alright, let's do this," Billy said without fear. The wind continued to increase, and the visibility decrease. Lightning was around us everywhere as we continued to get battered while crawling to the search area. We were all alone on this one, and there was nobody to rescue us if we got into trouble. While the NYPD had sent most of its assets away except for a few boats, FDNY and USCG had shut down their marine operations.

As we continued onward, I saw a flash of green lightning. "Did you see that?" I asked aloud to Billy and Brian as they ignored me. Then there was another flash of green lightning, and this time there was no way I was the only one who saw it. "Did you see that!?" I yelled, and they ignored me again. Out of the darkness came a large wave that hit us broadside, and I hit my head on the side of the cabin. My ears started ringing and everything went black as Billy forged ahead towards the first responder lights seen on land.

In the darkness after hitting my head, my body exited the boat and across Raritan Bay. I was floating peacefully above the ocean surface, surrounded by green lightning and rough seas. Waves were crashing against the rocks of Old Orchard Shoal Light in between Staten Island and New Jersey. There were two people in the water next to a half-sunken kayak not far away from the light. I could see what they were wearing as waves battered them. Another large wave hit Launch #311, and I was sucked back into my body as I came to from the hit on my head.

I got Billy's attention and yelled his name until he turned around to look at me. "What?!" he asked angrily. "We're going the wrong way," I replied. "What do you mean, I'm heading to where the lights are!" he yelled back. "No, no. They're not going to be over there. They're going to be over here!" I yelled while pointing to the south/southwest. He stared at me for what-felt-like a minute before saying, "Fine! We'll fucking do it your way!" All the anger Billy felt about me over the years came rushing back, but he turned the wheel hard to port, and we began slowly heading in the direction I pointed to.

Heading the way we were, we also got a better vantage point of the storm as it sent big walls of black water in our direction. The heavy swells seemed to run perfectly in between Rockaway and Sandy Hook, as wind waves piled up on top of the swells. It looked and felt like death as we slowly made our way to wherever my vision was taking us. The rain got even harder and the winds stronger with each passing minute as Irene's fury was getting closer.

"I see them! I see them!" Billy yelled out. "Where?" Brian asked. "Right there off of the bow!" Billy exclaimed as he pointed in their direction. In nearly 80 square miles of water, plus more if our victims had been taken out to sea, the bow of our boat went right into them. They were wearing exactly what I saw in my vision. It was an incredible moment, and we were all in disbelief. "How did you do that? How did you know?" Billy asked me in a puzzled tone. I shrugged my shoulders and then he said, "Let's get them out of the water." "Alright, let's do it!" Brian and I yelled at the same time.

We opened the hatches and doors of Launch #311 to go out into the elements. Brian went out onto the bow without any rails to hold onto. I opened the rear door to get to the stern and was immediately hit by a large wave. It washed over the rear deck and my legs, nearly knocking me down. I handed Brian a pike pole so that he could lower it into the water, have the victims grab it, and guide them toward me at the stern.

The plan worked initially, and we got the first victim in using our strategy. We brought him onto the boat and told him to go inside the cabin. The second one was a little bit more of a challenge. He was about 20ft away from us and astern on the starboard side of Launch #311. The wind was pushing us away from him as he struggled in the water. Billy also had to make sure a wave didn't capsize us, so it was hard to bring the boat about to get the last victim.

Billy tried to "split the sticks" to swing the ass of the boat into him, but the wind and wave action was too strong. He was a 55' boat pilot and was used to the controls of the larger vessels, while rarely using the smaller boats. On boats with inboard motors, you can split the throttles and steer it like a tank, but outboard motors have less bite and can't maneuver in conditions like that. "Don't split the sticks!" I yelled at him loud enough to overcome the roar of the wind and sound of crashing waves. Billy listened and we came about the traditional way to complete the rescue.

While the first victim was cooperative and helped us get him in, the other one was more worried about his half-sunken kayak and cell phone. Billy got Launch #311 as close as he could without the danger of crushing him if we got hit by a wave, but we needed his help, and I asked him to swim to me. "Swim to me! C'mon!" I yelled at him. "My boat!" he yelled back while looking away and holding a Ziplock bag in the air. The Ziplock bag contained a cell phone, and the phone was sloshing around the bag half-filled with water. "Forget about the fucking boat! It's gone!" I yelled back at him. "You gotta come to me now!" I screamed as a new set of squalls moved in and the wind roared.

He swam over to the cutout on the starboard side, and I dragged him in. They were both safely on board, shivering and battered. We closed the hatches and proceeded to scream at them for being so stupid. They apologized profusely and thanked us for saving their lives. Billy looked at me, still in shock that we found them somehow and made the rescue. "Let's get out of this and get to Great Kills," I said to him. "Right," Billy replied and grabbed the mic of the radio. "Launch 311 to central, we have the 2 kayakers on board. Show us going to Great Kills," he said while still bewildered.

Great Kills was the harbor in Staten Island, and with the weather the way it was, we still had a 15 minute ride out of danger. Large swells and strong winds pushed across the stern as our risk of capsizing increased, not decreased. While we slowly made our way over to the harbor, it hit us what we were part of in terms of the size and scope. Billy and Brian didn't know what I saw or what happened to me on the ride there, but they still knew that we were part of a miracle. Nobody in the NYPD had ever done anything like this before.

As we entered Great Kills Harbor, the seas flattened out to a minor chop. Wind still buffeted the boat, but we knew we were out of danger. The waves crashing against the rocks of Old Orchard Shoal Light kept replaying in my mind. I couldn't believe how incredible the waves were in Raritan Bay. The green light which was with me on-and-off throughout the years, had returned during the most dangerous moment in my life.

Billy did an incredible job that night, and this couldn't have happened without all of us being on the boat together. This is the way it had to be. For those young men to be saved that night, a crew was put together by forces beyond our comprehension. If I were at Croton-on-Hudson, I wouldn't have been there to show Billy where the victims were. If the pilot was me or anyone else, neither they nor I would've had the tenacity or skill to deal with that type of storm. If we didn't collectively say "no" to the order to turn around, another crew would've listened, leaving the victims for dead.

In the modern-day history of the NYPD Harbor Unit, no boat had ever gone out into a hurricane to make a rescue, until now. We were part of something huge, and these were all the things going through our heads as we pulled up to the docks safely. EMTs were waiting at the dock to check out the victims we plucked out of the water, and the 3 of us Harbor guys finally had a moment to ourselves. We shook hands and gave each other hugs for job well done. During that time, the mayor was already informed of what happened, and our daring rescue was mentioned by him during one of his hurricane updates.

As we stood there in the cabin and out of the elements, my phone rang and interrupted our euphoria. Big Pants was back on the phone. "Make sure you write them summonses," he told me. Stunned that those were the first words out of his mouth, I replied, "We don't have any paperwork, we ran out to make the rescue." He gruffed something unintelligible and hung up on me. A few minutes later, we got another call from one of the other supervisors we called "Little Pants". We were told to have the victims stand by, and that summonses were being driven out to us.

I understood the powers-that-be wanted tickets written to the victims. They had risked the lives of first responders by putting themselves in that position. However, it shouldn't have been the focus at that very moment. Why would any of us have paperwork? Why would I? I wasn't even supposed to be out on the boat, and the other guys had no specified boat assigned to them before the rescue. It was a sign of things to come as office politics took over to try and erase what happened.

Chapter 30: The Aftermath

We returned to Harbor Charlie in Brooklyn after issuing our hand-delivered summonses, and being replaced by a new crew to stay with Launch #311. The water was too rough to attempt a return, so the boat stayed in Great Kills Harbor for next 2 days. In the meantime, Hurricane Irene cut through New York City, devastating interior parts of the Northeast.

Most of the guys received us well and gave us a lot of praise for the rescue, but you could feel a chill in the air from the back office. "Good job," Big Pants said before closing his door and disappearing. I returned to my post on the desk as if nothing transpired, and we rode out the rest of the storm with no other rescues coming over the air. It was a long night, and I couldn't wait to get home to get some much-needed sleep.

Over the course of the next few days, we were debriefed by DCPI (the NYPD's press wing) and told we were to be interviewed by a well-known columnist for one of the big local papers. It was a phone interview, and we were called into the back office to rehearse and talk about what to expect. When the phone conference began, Big Pants did most of the talking, and we barely got a word in. The columnist was picking up on it, and he interrupted him to ask us some questions; then Big Pants started talking again.

He said something to the effect of going out there and doing your duty. Yet, he was the one of the guys who left us for dead and ordered us to turn around as well. It was a very awkward moment as we looked at him, then at each other, puzzled with the words he chose. As the interview came to an end, the columnist thanked us for a job well done. Big Pants hung up the phone and said to us, "It wasn't that bad out," before telling us to close the door as we left the back office.

We were stunned, but we understood what was going on. We disregarded that order to turn around and made a successful rescue. The back office was "circling the wagons" to protect itself. There was also fear that the high-profile nature of the rescue, might get the pilot and myself (Brian was already a detective) our detective shields as a reward for a job-well-done. It was customary for the NYPD to promote certain cops to "detective specialist" if they got into something high profile and noteworthy.

The Harbor Unit itself also had a peppering of detective specialists due to the specific skill set it took to run the big boats. Because of this, it attracted negative attention from those waiting to get promoted, and it became a very smarmy environment. So much so, that one of the administrative cops in the back office awaiting his promotion, started planting seeds that we were exaggerating about what happened out there. "It wasn't that bad" was the narrative he and others chose to run with. The supervisors even went as far as purposely not filling out the standard report when a rescue is made.

Life went on, though, and the good deeds continued to pile up. In September, my steady partner, K-Fed, finally got his first "big" rescue with me. We had rescued 2 deer found underneath the Verrazano Bridge while going out to post. When we plucked them out of the water, one of the yearlings kicked the crap out of K-Fed on the rear deck of the boat. For the next few months, I would

THE AFTERMATH

sneeze constantly because deer hair got into every nook and cranny of the boat.

Come October, I found myself on the 4th and last air disaster of that notorious stretch. An overloaded chopper had crashed into the East River after takeoff. Once again, we rushed up there from Jamaica Bay to assist. While not as physically gruesome as the plane/helicopter collision we had in Hoboken, it was still a rough scene with fatalities. In the aftermath, one of the high-ranking chiefs came up to me, and asked about the rescue we made during Hurricane Irene. I told him all about it without getting into too much detail and he said, "Write it up, I want it on my desk." "Write it up" meant to fill out the paperwork for a departmental recognition (medal).

The rescue was something that rose to a specific level, and they wanted it on their desk to push it forward. At the time, the "higher ups" were thinking this should be an "Honorable Mention" medal. After that, it would go in front of a board of "super chiefs" to see if it would warrant the NYPD Medal for Valor. I followed the chief's order, wrote up the paperwork, and we were hit with immediate resistance.

When I handed in the paperwork for the medals, I was told, "You can't hand it in like this," as Little Pants hinted it was all a lie. "Rewrite it and hand it back in," he told me. They didn't like what was written because it talked about the size of the seas, the winds, and how the other boat turned around with Big Pants in it.

I kept the original but handed in a new write-up which left out some of the details. Even then, the paperwork went nowhere for a few years as it sat on their desk. It was blatant and disgusting, but that's how the job works sometimes. It's what my dad was trying to protect me from when he said he'd "break my legs" if I became a cop. The moment had come and gone, and the miracle we took part in, may as well have not even happened.

During December of 2011, K-Fed found himself on another rescue with me. We wound up rescuing a dog and his owner in the icy waters of the Hudson River. We were at North Cove Marina when a dog rescue came over the air. A guy was playing fetch with his dog on the docks where the Titanic was supposed to pull into. The frisbee skipped into the water, the dog went after the frisbee, and the owner went in after the dog. We happened to be just minutes away from where the call came in, and we found them under the pier, clinging onto one of the pilings.

It was a dangerous rescue as we had to put the bow of the boat under the pier to get to the victim and his dog. Any wake caused by a local ferry boat, would've crushed the boat underneath the pier. K-Fed went onto bow and got the dog noose around the dog, pulling the dog onto the boat. Then we got the man into the boat and put them both in the heated cabin to prevent hypothermia. We were once again in the news, to the chagrin of others.

As for Jenn, she was told in late summer of 2012 that we could start trying for kids. We had set up this beautiful trip to St Augustine, FL and Savannah, GA to celebrate and start trying. When we got to Savannah, I looked at her as we were both sitting on the bed at the hotel. The sunlight shining through the thin curtains hit her face, and there was something different about her appearance. I said to myself, "She's pregnant." It turned out that I was right and she happened to get pregnant before we "officially" started trying on our vacation.

A few weeks after we returned from being away, Hurricane Sandy was waiting for us. We evacuated Long Beach once again, but the house was not spared as in Hurricane Irene. A pregnant Jenn, on bedrest due to medical complications, kissed me goodbye from her parent's house in East Meadow. She told me once more not to do anything stupid. I assured her that this time I'd be at Croton-on-Hudson all night long to safeguard the boats. My

THE AFTERMATH

partners and I were split up again, and this time I was far away from the action.

During the evening of the storm and to my surprise, a crew came to relieve some of us at the sheltered marina. We were supposed to be on the boats all night, but the new crew arrived so that we could go home. When we got back to Harbor Charlie, it looked as if Godzilla had stepped on the base, and all the docks were destroyed. They had all evacuated to the Brooklyn Army Terminal, with the base in ruins.

Once again, I found myself breaking a promise to Jenn and going back out when a cop went missing in Staten Island. I volunteered to go out into Sandy's wrath with 2 SCUBA guys. Our mission was to search for the missing cop in the floodwater surrounding his home. My 2 SCUBA partners found the missing officer, but they were unable to get to him because the floodwater was electrified. While evacuating his family from the house, he had been electrocuted going downstairs one more time to look for any remaining family. We had to leave his body behind, and it was one of the worst feelings I ever had on this job.

After we had no choice but to leave the deceased officer, we were called to the ESU Truck 5 base. A woman and her children were swept away by the storm surge, and they needed us to help look for them. As we got our assignment and left for the search, water began rushing down Hylan Boulevard while trying to make our way towards New Dorp Beach and Oakwood in Staten Island. Everywhere we turned there was water. In some cases, the surge was so extreme, you would be face-to-face with traffic lights if on a boat.

The SCUBA guys went out into the dark with an inflatable boat to search for the mom and her kids. I stood by with the truck, wondering if my partners were alright. The radios had died, and all the power was out. I had no idea where they were. As I waited for them to return, victims of the flood were sloshing through the water towards me in the darkness. One by one, I'd take them to higher ground with the truck, then return and wait for the SCUBA guys. About an hour later, they came back empty-handed, and it was time to pack things up.

However, our night wasn't over yet. We got called to assist in Breezy Point, Queens after a gas explosion leveled most of the town. A 3rd storm surge was heading in, and they needed our help. As we drove back over the Verrazano Bridge to get to the Rockaways, we looked to the southeast and you could see an orange glow as if the place got nuked. Upon arrival, we loaded up victims into large trucks which took them to safety.

Little Pants came up to me and started doing the math in his head, knowing I had been up at Croton-on-Hudson. "How long have you been working?" he asked. I looked at him and shrugged my shoulders. "You're done," he said while ordering me to go home. My night had come to an end right there. After working more than 20 hours straight in Hurricane Sandy and making countless rescues with my partners, I came home, gave Jenn a kiss, and slept for 13 hours. There was a lot to be done, a lot to rebuild, and a lot of uncertainty ahead for Jenn and the baby.

In the end, Hurricane Sandy made Irene look like nothing. The miracle we were part of was lost forever due to office politics, skullduggery, and Sandy's shadow. However, Sandy did leave one gift for us as she annihilated the city. During the rescue in Hurricane Irene, I was able to tell the size of the waves based on what I saw crashing up against Old Orchard Shoal Light. The back office insinuated that we were exaggerating, and that it was "impossible" that the waves could be that big in Raritan Bay. Hurricane Sandy wound up shearing the 100+ year old, 35ft high iron structure, clean off the rocks; proving that we were telling the truth all along. In a few months, none of it would matter anyway.

Chapter 31: Little Fire

During the time window between Hurricane Sandy and the recovery effort that ensued, Jenn almost lost the baby twice due to a medical condition. With her age and auto-immune disease considered, the risks were very high, and she was being monitored very closely. The doctors decided to run some tests. At the only appointment I couldn't attend due to work, they told her that the baby had a problem with its heart. She called me at work and was sobbing over the phone. I felt so helpless as I was out in the middle of nowhere on the boat and couldn't help. Not being there for her, even if it were just that one time, is something that still bothers me to this day.

Throughout the next few months, the doctors did genetic testing and more scanning to get a better look at the heart. During the genetic testing process, we found out that we were having a boy. While Jenn was initially scared to have kids, she always wanted a boy if she decided to have a family. She even had a name picked out a very long time ago, and if it were a boy, he was to be named, Aiden. Aiden means "Little Fire" in Gaelic, and I thought it was a great name.

As we neared April of 2013, the news was not good for Aiden, and there were no improvements with his heart. We were told that the prospects were very high that he would need open heart surgery during the first 6 months of his life. Jenn and I were devastated and didn't know what to do. Our baby was going to need so much help, and I wasn't sure how we were going to handle it when factoring in the NYPD.

Jenn was fine schedule-wise and had a lot of support over at Special Ops. I was in a toxic environment where favors didn't come cheap or often, and I was about to find that out. An appointment was made for me with Big Pants to ask for a different schedule temporarily. I had asked him if I could work 6pm-2am temporarily until the baby had his surgery and out of danger. Big Pants shook his head and said, "I can't, I need you on the boat." His denial wasn't anything personal; this is who he was. I stood up from my chair, thanked him for his time, and told him I had to look for a new assignment if he couldn't help me. His face turned red with anger, and he told me to close the door behind me when I left.

There was a big miscalculation on his part. I loved what I did in Harbor, and I loved being there. It was my dream assignment, and I was good at what I did. He mistook that feeling as a sign that I would "roll over" and do anything to stay. Some cops choose the job over family, especially if they're in a good assignment, but I was not one of them. I was fully prepared to walk away from one of the best assignments in the NYPD, to take care of my family.

The chief got wind of what was going on since Jenn worked at Special Ops, and they could see her struggling daily. I got a phone call from Special Ops a few nights after the episode with Big Pants. They told me I was being temporarily transferred there at the discretion of the chief to help Jenn. My time in Harbor was essentially over. I was heartbroken, but I had to do what was right for Jenn and Aiden. The patrol boat I was on returned me to the docks and dropped me off. I emptied my locker and left.

There were some adjustments to be made schedule-wise. The administrative staff had to do a "chart change" for me due to my rotating days off in Harbor vs. the steady days off at Special Ops. It afforded me a few extra days off after going there to set up my new locker and having a quick crash-course on my new assignment. Jenn was delighted to have me there since the new schedule would ensure her and Aiden were taken care of. With all the "wrongs" that had happened over the course of the last couple of years, the chief took notice and stepped in to do something right. He understood what was going on and the politics behind it, so he intervened to help my family.

On April 17, 2013, I was driving to the NYPD Special Ops base at Floyd Bennett Field in Brooklyn. It would be the first day of my first full week working there. Cigar in mouth, I cruised to work with the windows open and music playing. We had about 7 weeks left until Aiden arrived. Regardless of the worries ahead, I was in a relaxed state. Each day before my shift, I'd work a little bit on the baby room and get things ready for his arrival. I was making room for the crib that hadn't arrived yet, but there were no concerns since we had time.

I pulled up, walked into the building, and some familiar faces welcomed me. Jenn's original condition had resolved itself, so she was back at the base. She worked behind the desk in civilian clothes since her baby-bump was getting bigger. She smiled at me, and I introduced myself to those I didn't know yet. As I was talking, she walked out of the office and down the hallway. I noticed she had left but didn't think anything of it until she was gone for a while. When I opened the door to the hallway to go check on her, she was standing by the door, leaning up against the wall with a worried look on her face. "My water broke," she said as her eyes started to tear up.

On the inside, I was panicking, especially since it was so early. I also couldn't believe this was happening right now on my first day at Special Ops. I took a deep breath in, stopped myself from showing Jenn I was scared, and said, "Ok, let's go to the hospital." Everyone else was in a panic, especially the other guys as they all moved around the office like ping pong balls; bumping into each other and not knowing what to do. The lieutenant threw me the keys to an unmarked RMP and said, "Go." He also had another cop come with us.

When all this unfolded, it was dead-stop rush hour traffic on the Belt Parkway in the city. We needed to get Jenn to Manhasset, NY for her to receive the care she needed due to Aiden's heart. I put Jenn in the car, the other cop got into back seat, then I climbed into the driver's seat. I started the engine, looked at the cop in the back, and said in an elevated tone, "Hold on!" We flew out of the base and to the Belt Parkway, where we were met with gridlock traffic. The hospital was notified ahead, and the staff was expecting us.

Lights activated and sirens blaring, I weaved in and out of traffic using the shoulder and the center median at times. I was doing things to that car which well-exceeded the manufacturer's recommendations, but she did well as I squeezed it through narrow spots that didn't seem to fit. In some cases, we were 1/2" away from other side view mirrors when I flew by as fast as we could. All-in-all, we got from Brooklyn to Manhasset on the north shore of Long Island in about 25 minutes. I had to have broken some sort of time record getting there in the traffic we experienced.

We raced up to the emergency room entrance at a high rate of speed with the tires screeching. When I looked at the cop in the back seat, he was catatonic and ghost white from the ride. I opened the door for Jenn, threw the other cop the keys to the RMP, and we went inside. As we went in, a small crowd of people were looking at the car, stunned at how we made our entrance. I turned to look at the RMP, and it was smoldering as the smell of burning brakes and oil wafted everywhere.

Over the course of the next few hours, the hospital staff did everything they could to try and stop Jenn from delivering Aiden. They pumped her full of steroids to help his lungs just in case the other meds couldn't stop the labor. The plan was to have Jenn hold onto Aiden for a week in the hospital before giving birth. They were confident it would work, but they were wrong. He was coming and there was nothing anyone can do about it.

When there was nothing left they could do, the doctors decided to try and get Jenn to have natural childbirth. For hours Jenn tried, but he wasn't coming. My intuition told me there was something wrong and when I tried to tell the doctor, he looked at me as if I didn't know what I was talking about. "You're not a doctor!" he barked at me. It didn't matter to me as he tried to throw his title around; I knew something was wrong. I took him by his elbow gently, turned him my way, looked him dead in the eyes, and said, "Something is wrong, you have to get him out."

He stared back at me for a minute, looked at the nurse, and said, "Prepare the patient for surgery." Jenn looked at me defeated, scared, and in pain. However, I was 100% sure that this was the right call. With all the things guiding me throughout the years and Pat helping me learn to control it, I knew this was one of those moments something had to be done. They wheeled Jenn into the operating room and began to prepare her for an emergency C-section.

I sat next to Jenn and held her hand as they put up a curtain so that she couldn't see all her insides being taken out and put back together. I heard them working frantically, communicating with each other quickly as surgical instruments hit the metal trays. There was no sound of a baby crying, just movement of the doctors and the sense of urgency. I couldn't see what was going on because I tried to focus on Jenn and keep her calm. I had no idea what was happening, and I was getting worried.

"Mr. Reiver, here is your baby boy," a nurse said to me as she handed this perfect little baby over to me. He was very calm and quiet, wrapped in this tiny blanket and cap. I couldn't believe how small he was, but I was thankful he was alive. Jenn looked over and I gave her a kiss, then I stared back at Aiden. The meaning of his name, "Little Fire", became more than just symbolic. It was real life as he weighed in at just over 4lbs. His hands were the size of postage stamps, and his forearms were only as thick as my thumbs. Regardless of him being premature and having his heart issue, all the worries disappeared for a moment as he continued to stare at me.

Later, we found out that Jenn would've never been able to give birth to him naturally due to her body never fully adjusting to pregnancy. Aiden's umbilical cord was also tangled around his neck, adding to the complications when you factor in his heart and preemie status. When I heard the news, I closed my eyes and thanked God that I was there when Jenn's water broke. I'm not sure what would've happened if I had still been in the Harbor Unit and out on a boat. I was meant to be there and at that exact moment.

Jenn wound up coming home from the hospital before Aiden did. He spent the next week or so in the NICU as they monitored him closely. The doctors and nurses were making sure he was ok to go home before the next step. For the time being, the NYPD assigned me to my family so that I could run milk up to the hospital for Aiden, while taking care of Jenn at home. We had a very long road ahead and my new command at Special Ops was very accommodating.

Over the course of the next several months, feeding Aiden was very difficult due to his heart and his body overcompensating for the medical issues. We did the best we could to keep him strong enough and heavy enough for any potential surgery. He also had a new doctor appointment almost every week to keep a close eye on him. Their biggest concern was "failure to thrive" if he wasn't getting enough nutrition.

Because of his enlarged heart, eating was difficult due to it pushing on his other organs. Reflux was a major issue, and we could only feed him 1-2oz of milk/formula at a time. I set the alarm on my phone for every hour and a half to feed him a little bit at a time over the course of 24hrs. The schedule probably took years off my life, but I didn't care. He was the most important thing to me, and I didn't want to lose him.

Jenn's parents fell in love with Aiden the moment they first saw him. Everyone did as he had this perfect little face and was such a good baby with an infectious smile. Even Marble the Shih Tzu got in on the action, watching him closely as he slept in his rocker, car seat, or our arms. I knew how much her parents cared for him when we found out that Aiden needed open heart surgery in October that year. Jenn's father, Dan, was holding Aiden when we broke the news to him and he wept. I've never seen that man cry before and never did again.

I prayed constantly for Aiden to be ok and did everything I could to stay calm and focused on Jenn. I prayed for wisdom, strength, and guidance. I whispered to myself every night as my head hit the pillow. I even offered my life for his, anything to make sure he would make it through this dangerous surgery. The day had come, and we drove him up to the hospital.

It was almost 4 years ago when Jenn and I almost didn't make it over her fear of having children. She was afraid she didn't have the instinct to be a good mother. Now here we are, faced with the biggest test as a couple and new parents. The nurses came out and told us Aiden was ready to go into the operating room, but only one of us could take him into the back. Jenn scooped him up, held him tight in her arms, looked directly at me, and said, "I'm taking him in."

This was her moment, and Jenn was everything she thought she wasn't capable of being. This was her Hurricane Irene, her Hurricane Sandy, and her aircraft disaster. She bravely walked through the swinging doors, disappearing with Aiden into the blinding white light.

Epilogue

From the green orb which lifted me up and placed me back onto the bed as a baby, to the frightening green light miraculously healing my hands as a boy; the power of angels, the power of God, the power of *something*, is undeniable in my eyes. It is as real as the keyboard I'm typing on at this moment. My life was one filled with infinite paths. Yet, it took me on this semi-controlled journey despite mistakes, accidents, illness, and sorrow.

As the spirits haunt the streets and buildings of Rockaway and beyond, I am reminded that there is much more out there that is forward, backward, and sideways. With time and the Universe weaving an invisible web, somewhere there is a Ben who exists that was never healed or helped. There's a Ben who exists that never confronted his bullies, never got switched to another school, and never got into the accident.

There could even be a Ben out there who died because he didn't put his lap belt on, or paying child support and eating ramen noodles in a basement apartment; all because he wasn't brave enough to walk away from an unhappy relationship. There could be a version of me who listened to the naysayers and didn't get back into the boxing ring, never becoming a cop, meeting Jenn, or having Aiden.

I know for a fact there's a version of me out there who was a cop during September 11th at the site of the attack. Not only due to the horrible dreams, but because of my dad's old commanding officer, Bernie Weber. He would always talk to me about being a cop before my accident. Bernie tried to drive it into my mind that Manhattan was the place to work as a young, single man. His roots were in the 1st Precinct. He wanted me there, which is where the attack took place.

ANGEL OF THE STORM

The endless paths and possibilities go on and on. Had I gone back to the celebrity's apartment on New Year's Eve or listened to my supervisor's order to turn around in Hurricane Irene, things would not be the same today. That's because life is all about choices. It's about following that intuition inside of you, pursuing the things you enjoy, fighting for what you believe in, fighting for the people you love, or knowing when to walk away from something toxic. It's about recognizing when an invisible hand is coming down to guide you out of danger or using you as His instrument to help others in a spectacular miracle.

Stopping, thinking, pausing, listening, and doing, always winds up with better results than going against the grain of the Universe. Being different, not following the crowd, and having integrity, will not win you a lot of friends, but it will lead to a more rewarding life in the big picture. I know this as many people still don't understand me, and that's something I've accepted. I've learned to ignore the noise as should you. This is what Pat taught me, and this is why I am still here for the time being.

It's about recognizing how souls intentionally intersect and interact with one another for specific reasons. They're sent to help you, or you to help them. They prompt you to get off your ass and act, like my friend Sagee encouraging me to write this book. Sometimes they're even put back into your lives for a flash-in-the-pan experience to teach you something; like the time I ran back into celebrity chef, Anthony Bourdain. A chance photo taken by me of a bottle of Scotch in a snowstorm, got me a private dinner with him somehow.

The Scotch distillery was collaborating with him on a project and had invited a handful of people for dinner. They had a seat available, and their social media director invited me after giving them permission to use my photo. When Mr. Bourdain approached me, I told him how Jenn and I were sitting next to him at JFK

EPILOGUE

airport 4 years prior. "How come you didn't say anything?" he asked. "Because we didn't want to bother you," I replied. "That's a good man," the typically grumpy chef said with a smile. We went on to have a great conversation amongst two very different men for a moment. It's something I'll never forget; how precious life is, how magical it can be if you just allow it, and how swiftly it can be taken from us.

Regarding precious life, Aiden survived his surgery after two failed attempts to restart his heart. It took a long time for him to recover from everything, but he is a healthy boy in middle school now. I wound up staying at NYPD Special Operations, and they did everything they could so that we could take care of him. This is the way life had to be, even with all the negativity and setbacks at times. Everything happened in the order it was supposed to. It was so that my son could come into this world and be protected. He cried when he read this passage, because he understands the gravity of it all, and how blessed he is to be part of an amazing story.

One day when Aiden was a toddler, we were all sitting on our bed as a family. Aiden began to tell us a story about a green light that visited him the night before. When I asked him what it was, he used his hands to describe a light the size of a tennis ball weaving in and out of the covers.

The "Angel of the Storm" is with Aiden now, watching over him. May God help him if he wants to be a cop. I'll break his legs.

www.ingramcontent.com/pod-product-compliance
Lightning Source LLC
Chambersburg PA
CBHW020247010526
44107CB00002B/134